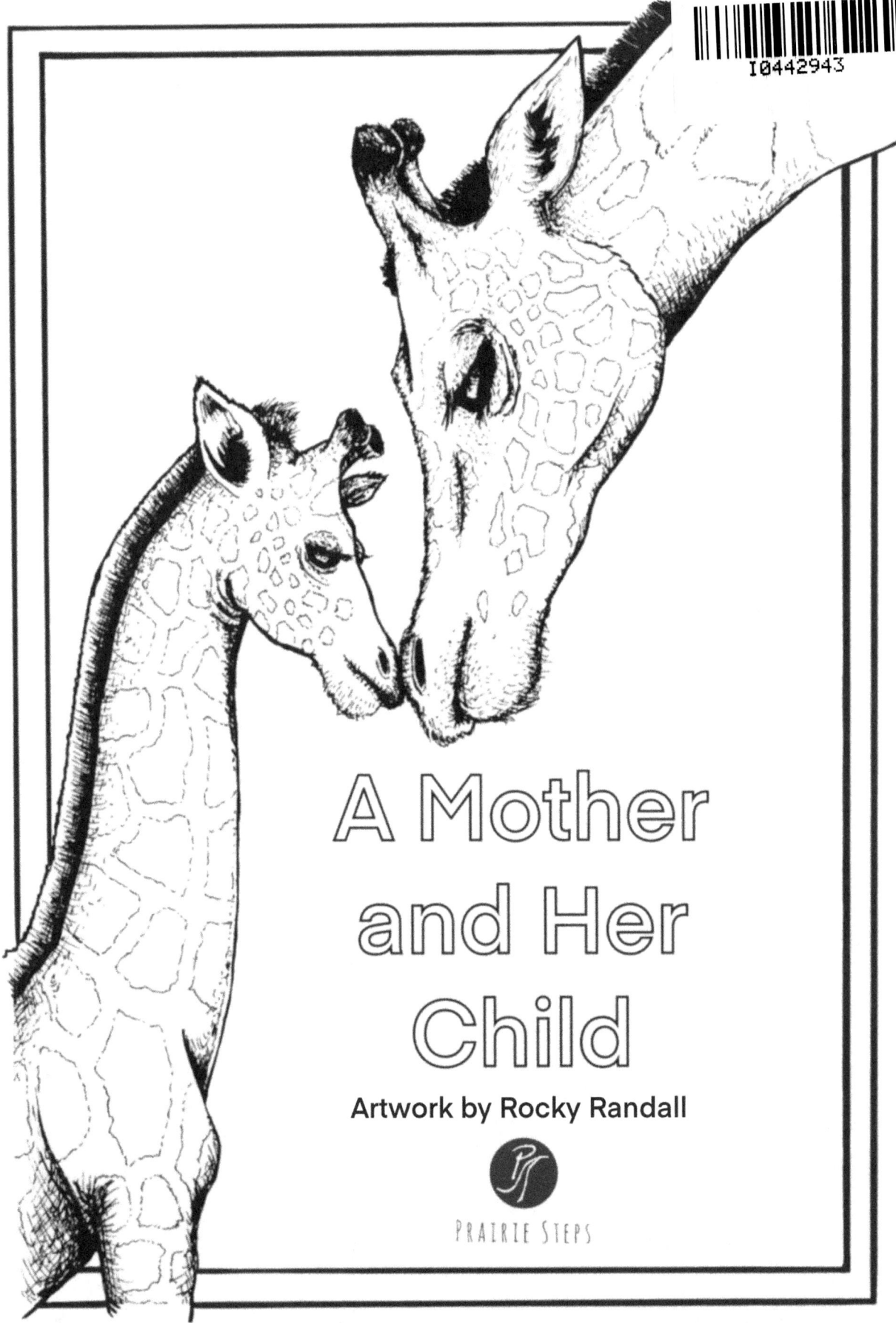

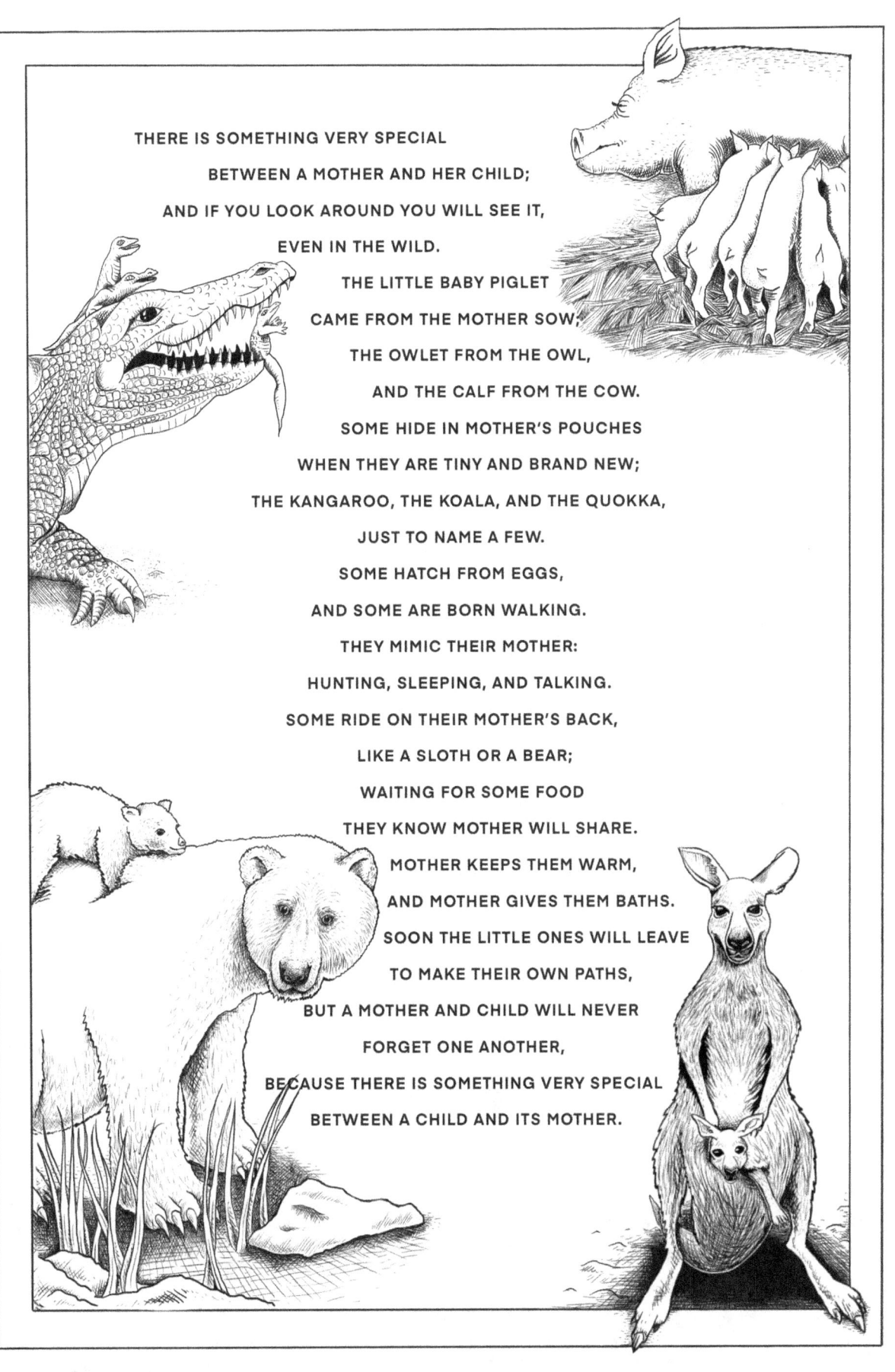

THERE IS SOMETHING VERY SPECIAL
BETWEEN A MOTHER AND HER CHILD;
AND IF YOU LOOK AROUND YOU WILL SEE IT,
EVEN IN THE WILD.
THE LITTLE BABY PIGLET
CAME FROM THE MOTHER SOW;
THE OWLET FROM THE OWL,
AND THE CALF FROM THE COW.
SOME HIDE IN MOTHER'S POUCHES
WHEN THEY ARE TINY AND BRAND NEW;
THE KANGAROO, THE KOALA, AND THE QUOKKA,
JUST TO NAME A FEW.
SOME HATCH FROM EGGS,
AND SOME ARE BORN WALKING.
THEY MIMIC THEIR MOTHER:
HUNTING, SLEEPING, AND TALKING.
SOME RIDE ON THEIR MOTHER'S BACK,
LIKE A SLOTH OR A BEAR;
WAITING FOR SOME FOOD
THEY KNOW MOTHER WILL SHARE.
MOTHER KEEPS THEM WARM,
AND MOTHER GIVES THEM BATHS.
SOON THE LITTLE ONES WILL LEAVE
TO MAKE THEIR OWN PATHS,
BUT A MOTHER AND CHILD WILL NEVER
FORGET ONE ANOTHER,
BECAUSE THERE IS SOMETHING VERY SPECIAL
BETWEEN A CHILD AND ITS MOTHER.

Pigs
A SOW AND HER PIGLETS

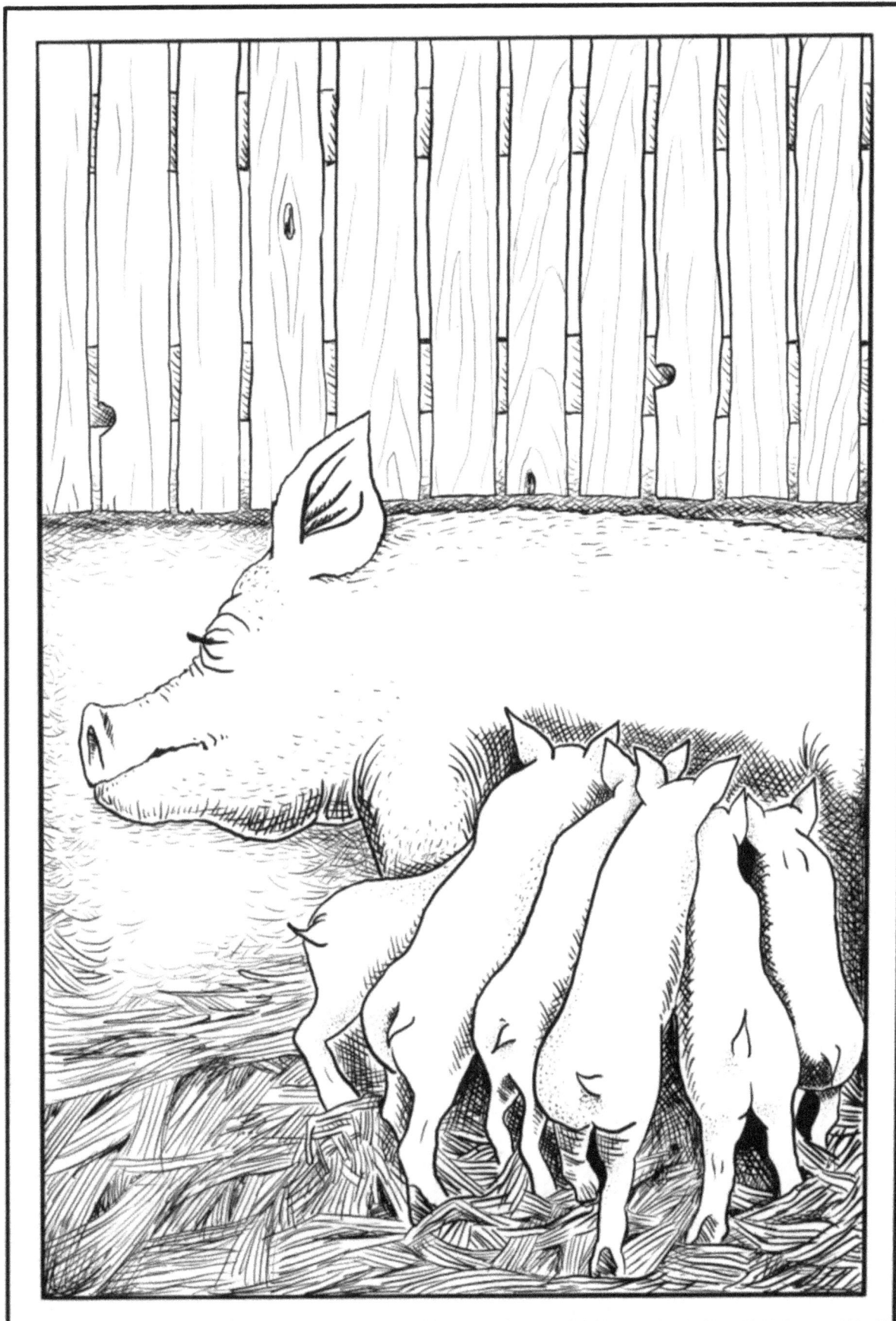

Horses
A DAM AND HER FOAL

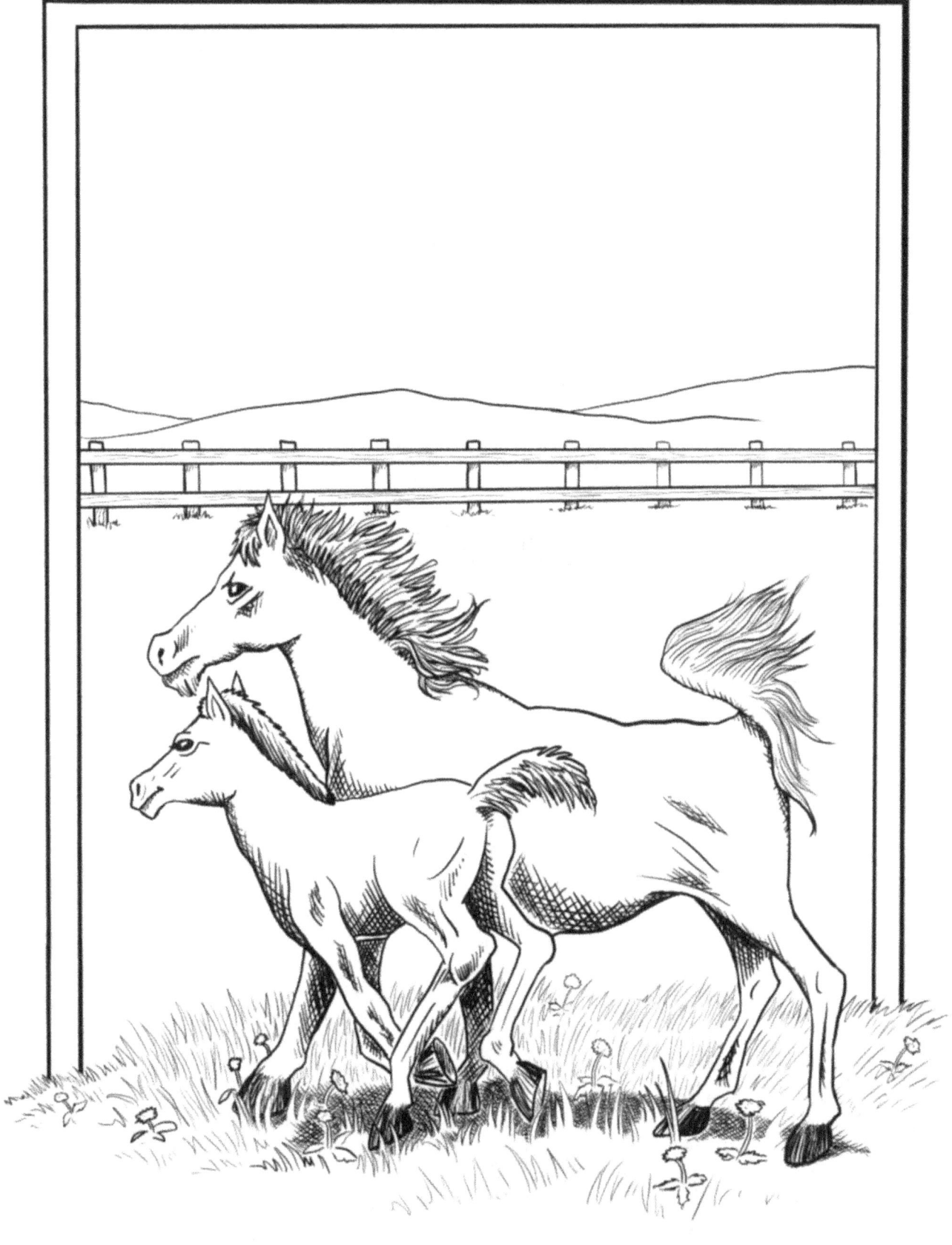

Deer
A DOE AND HER FAWN

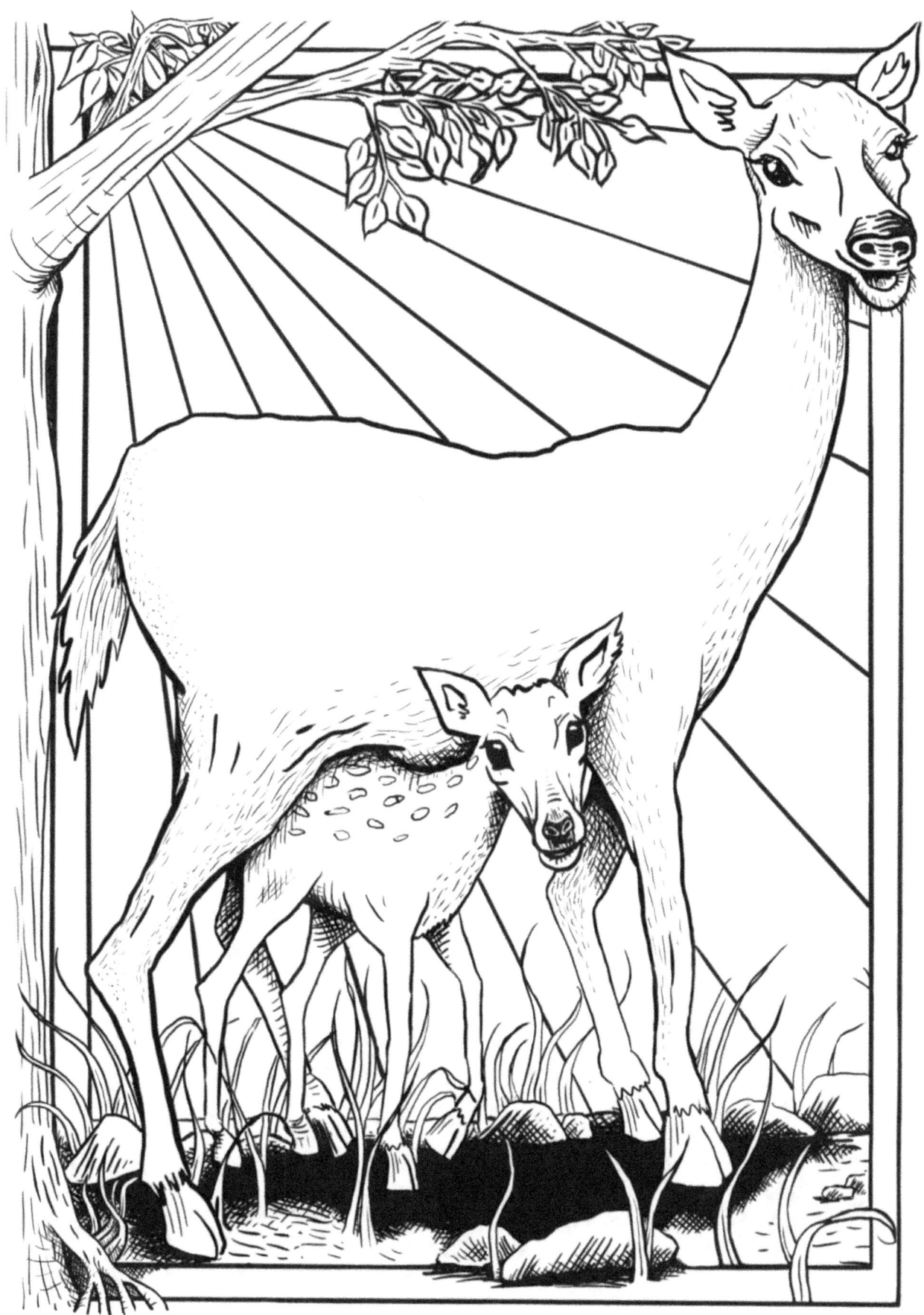

Dogs
A DAM AND HER PUP

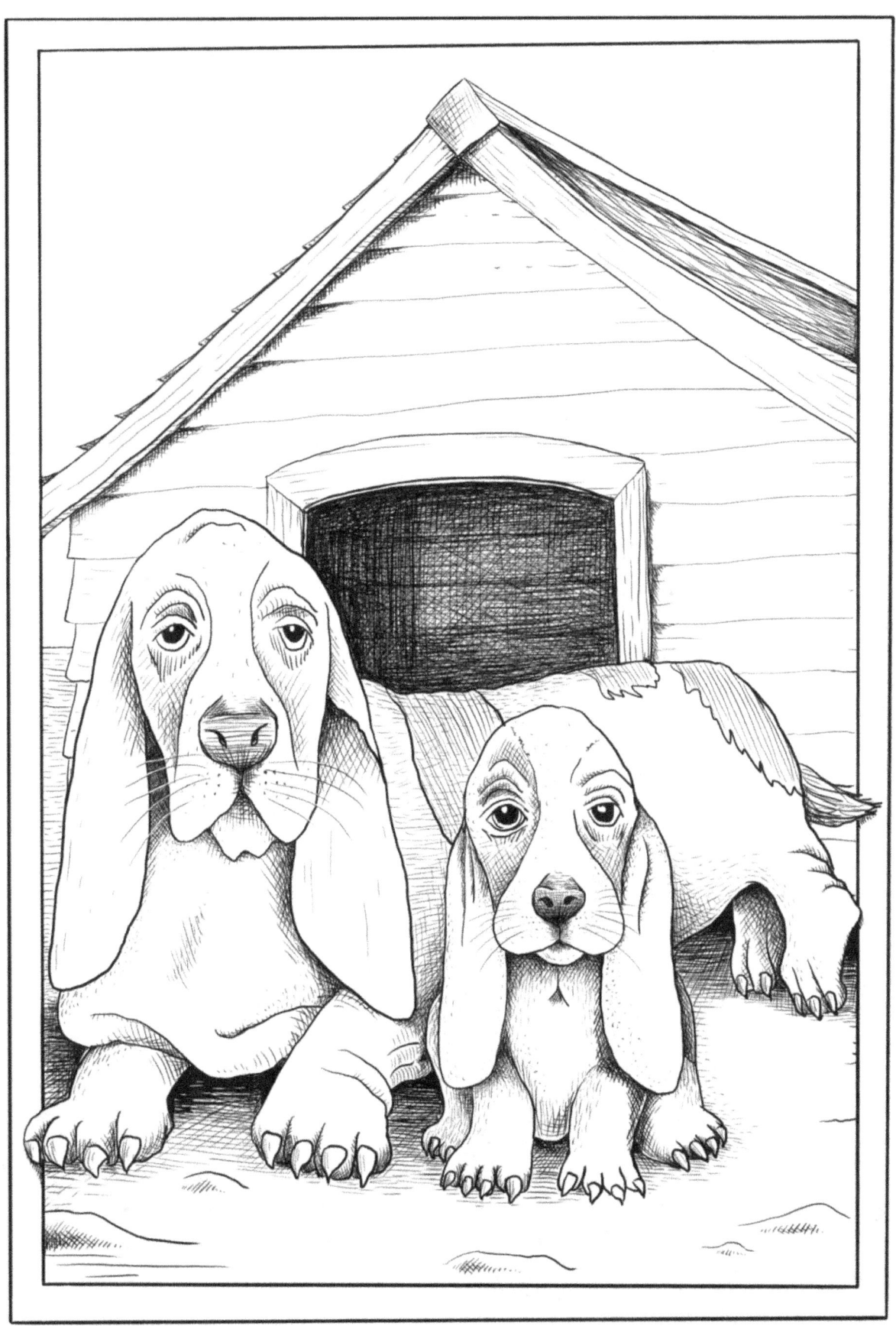

Coyotes
A COYOTE AND HER PUPS

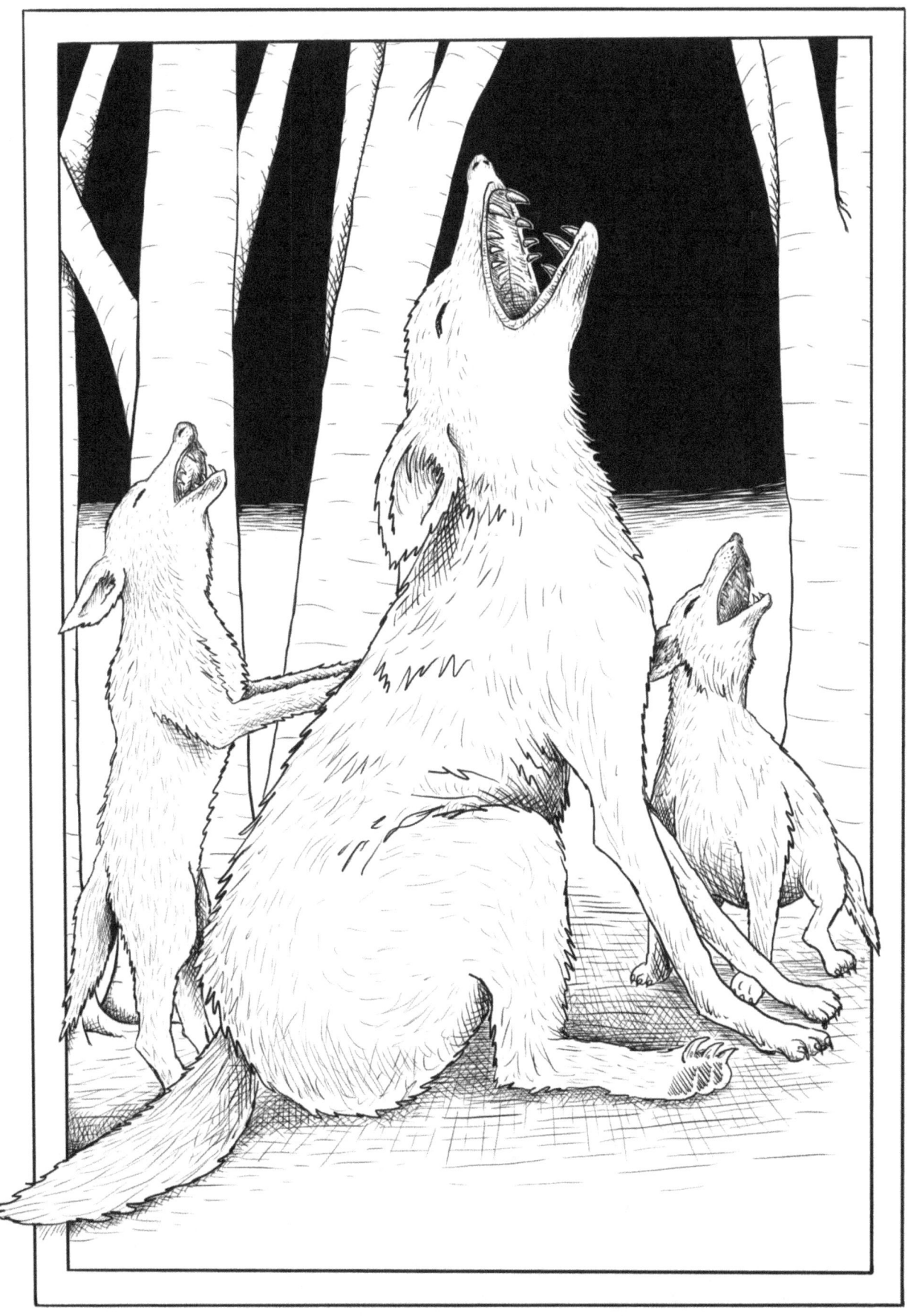

Spiders

A SPIDER AND HER SPIDERLINGS

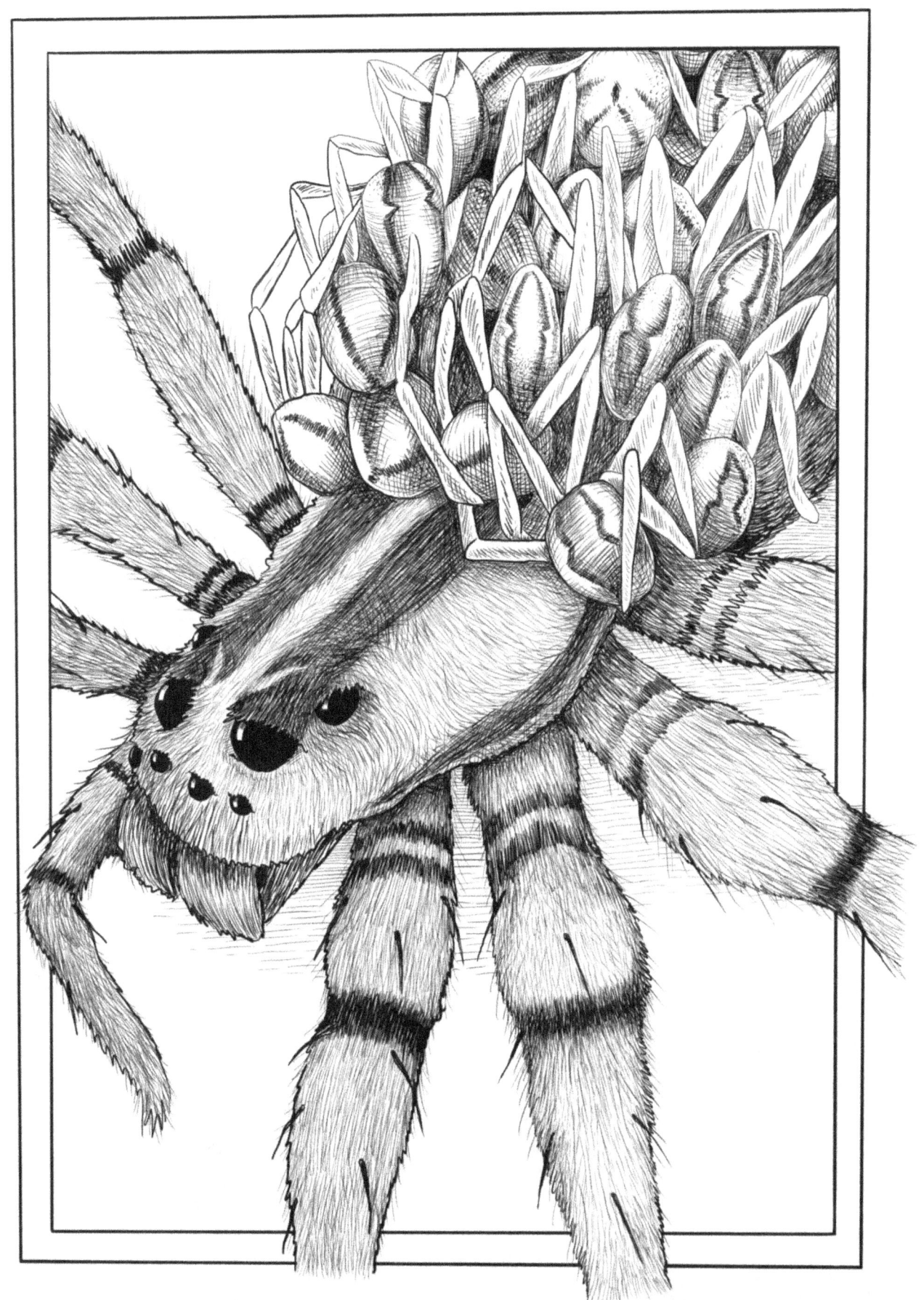

Chickens
A HEN AND HER CHICKS

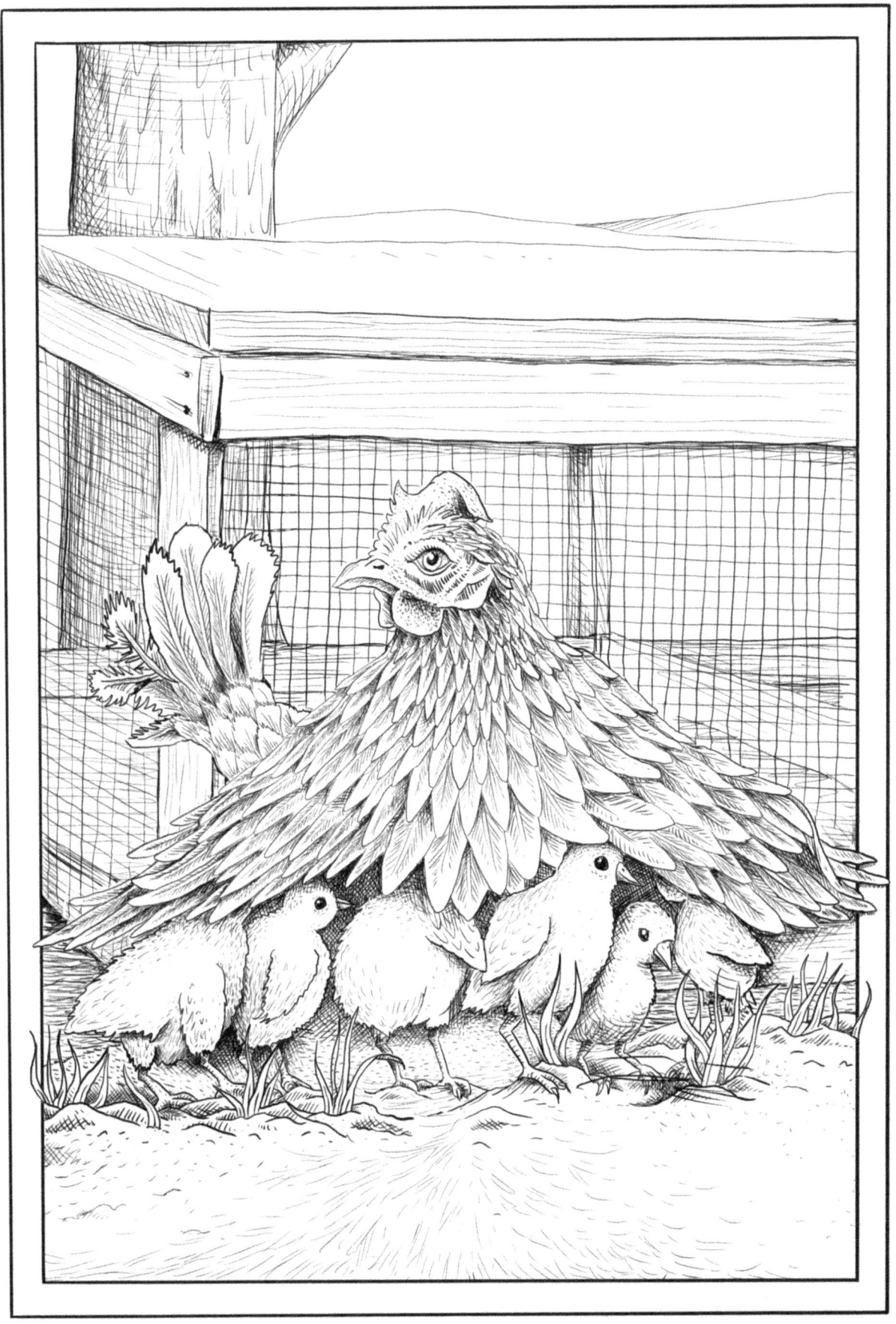

Bears
A SOW AND HER CUB

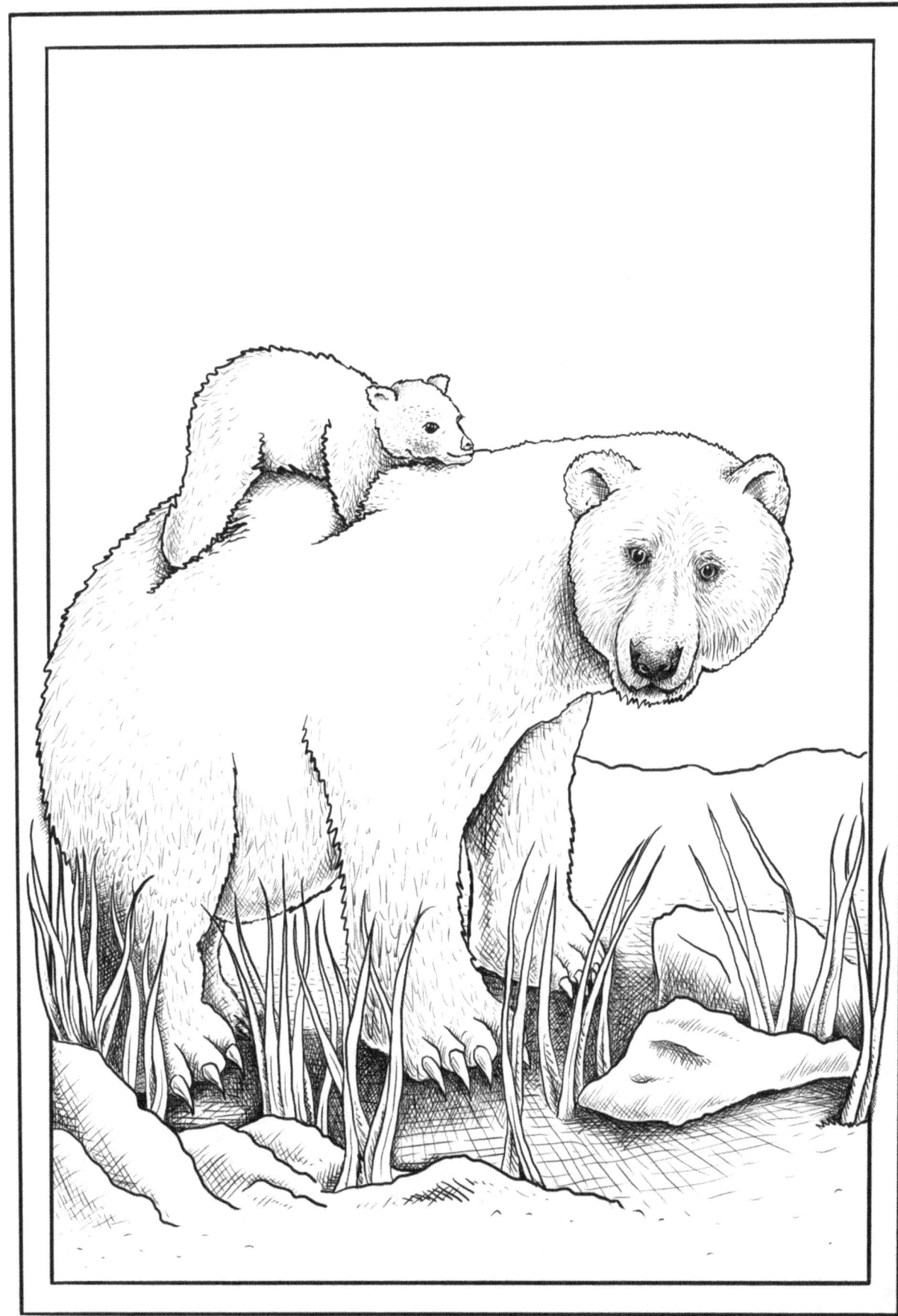

Owls
AN OWL AND HER HATCHLING

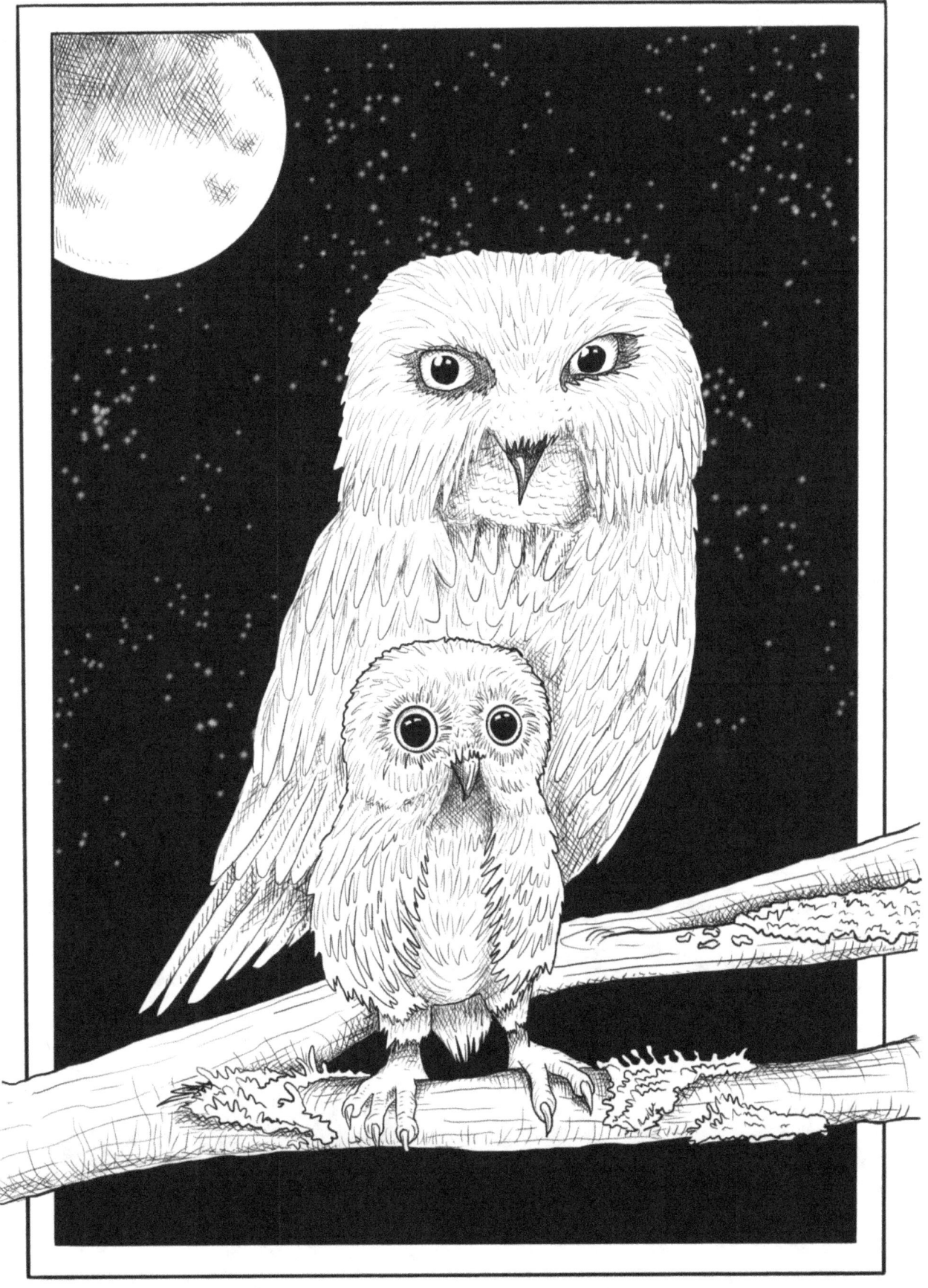

Mice
A DOE AND HER PINKIES

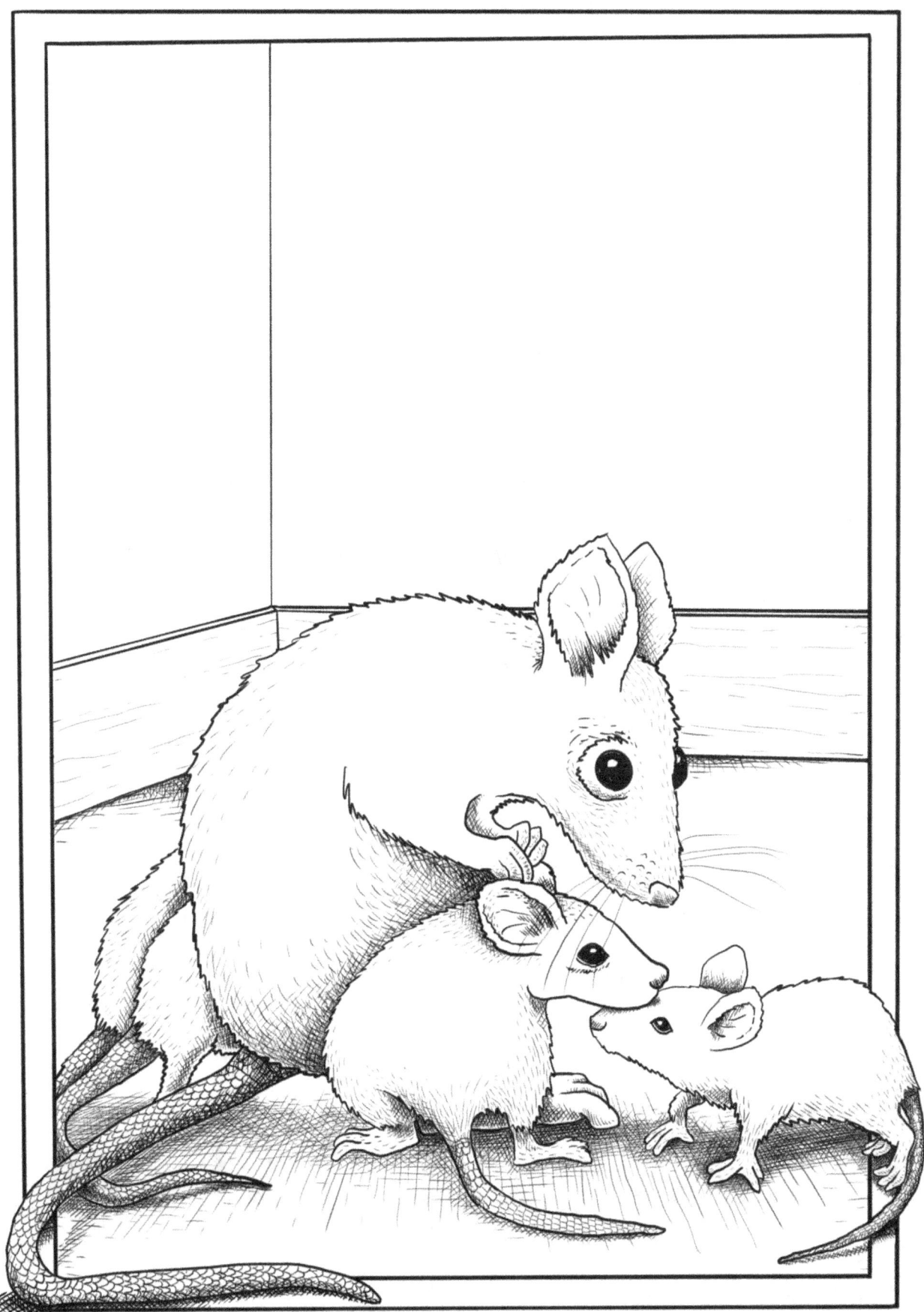

Tigers

A TIGRESS AND HER CUB

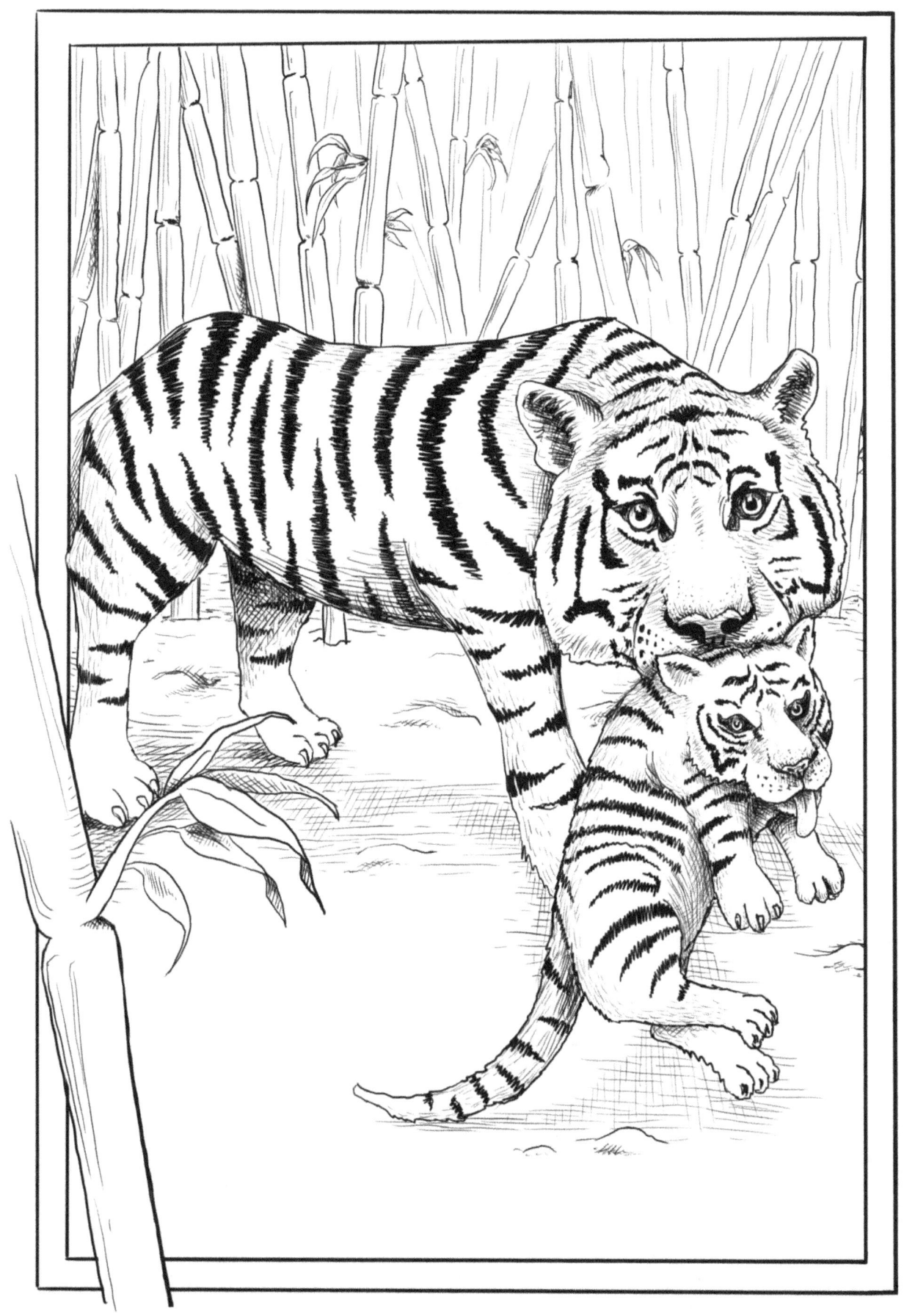

Sharks
A SHARK AND HER PUP

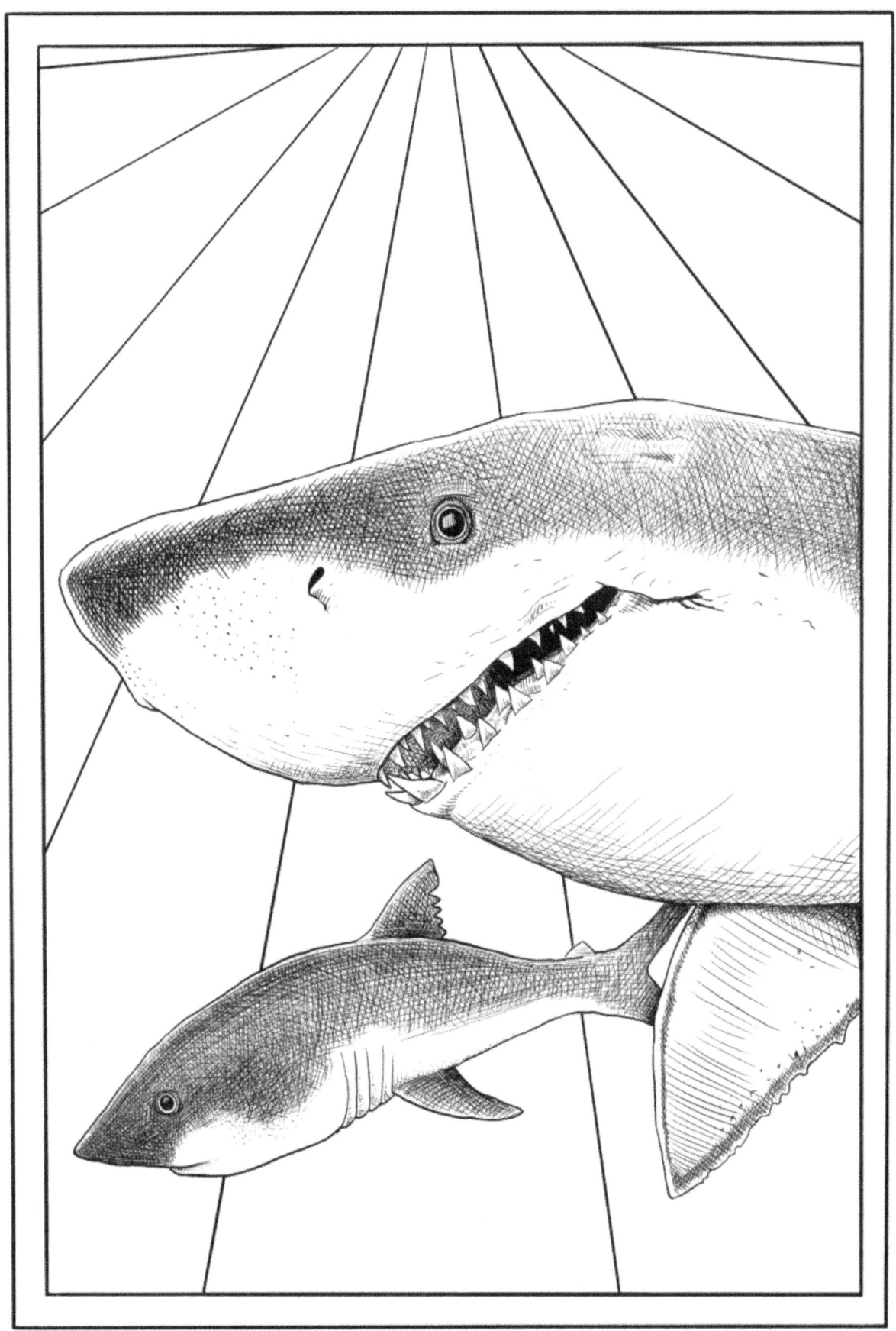

Turtles
A TURTLE AND HER HATCHLING

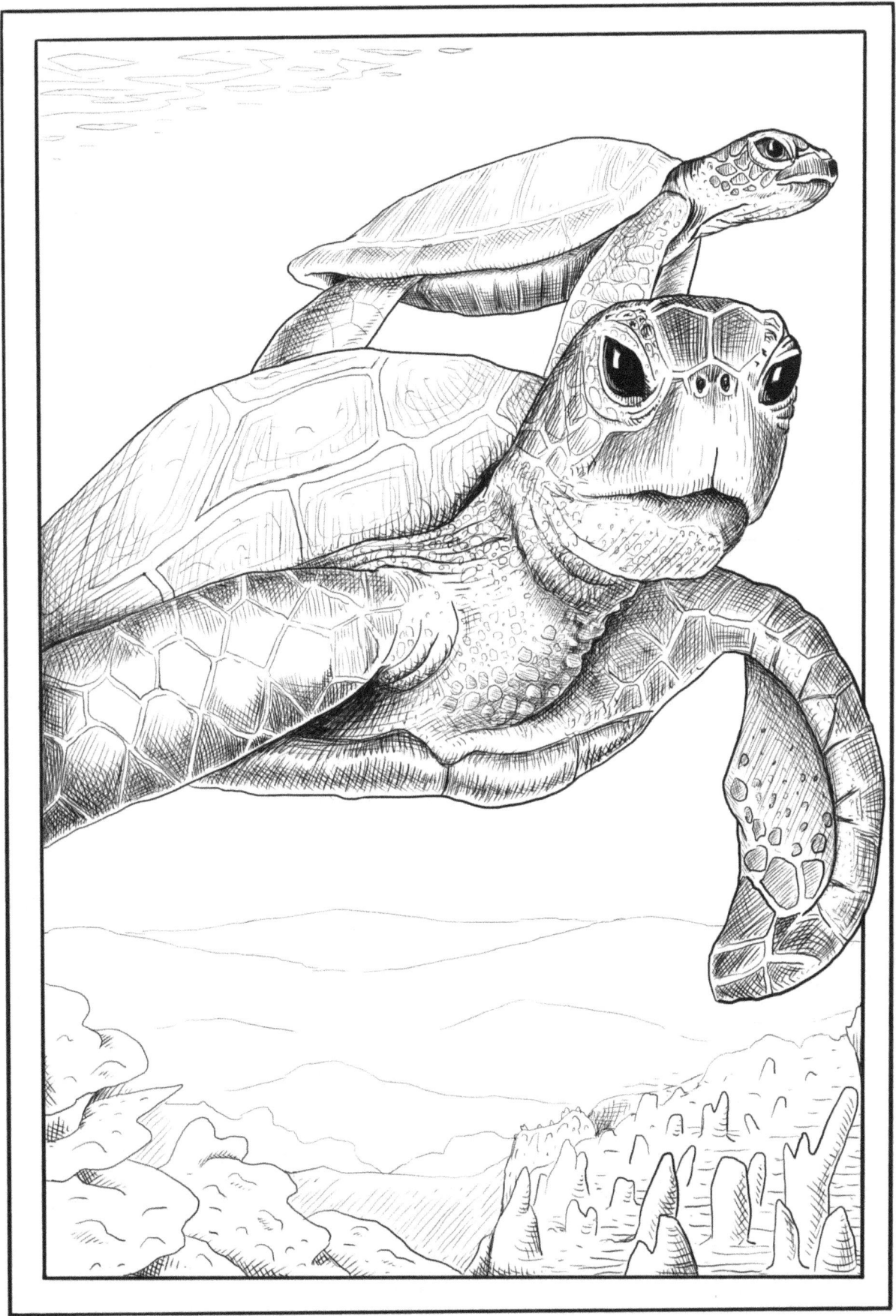

Crocodiles
A COW AND HER HATCHLINGS

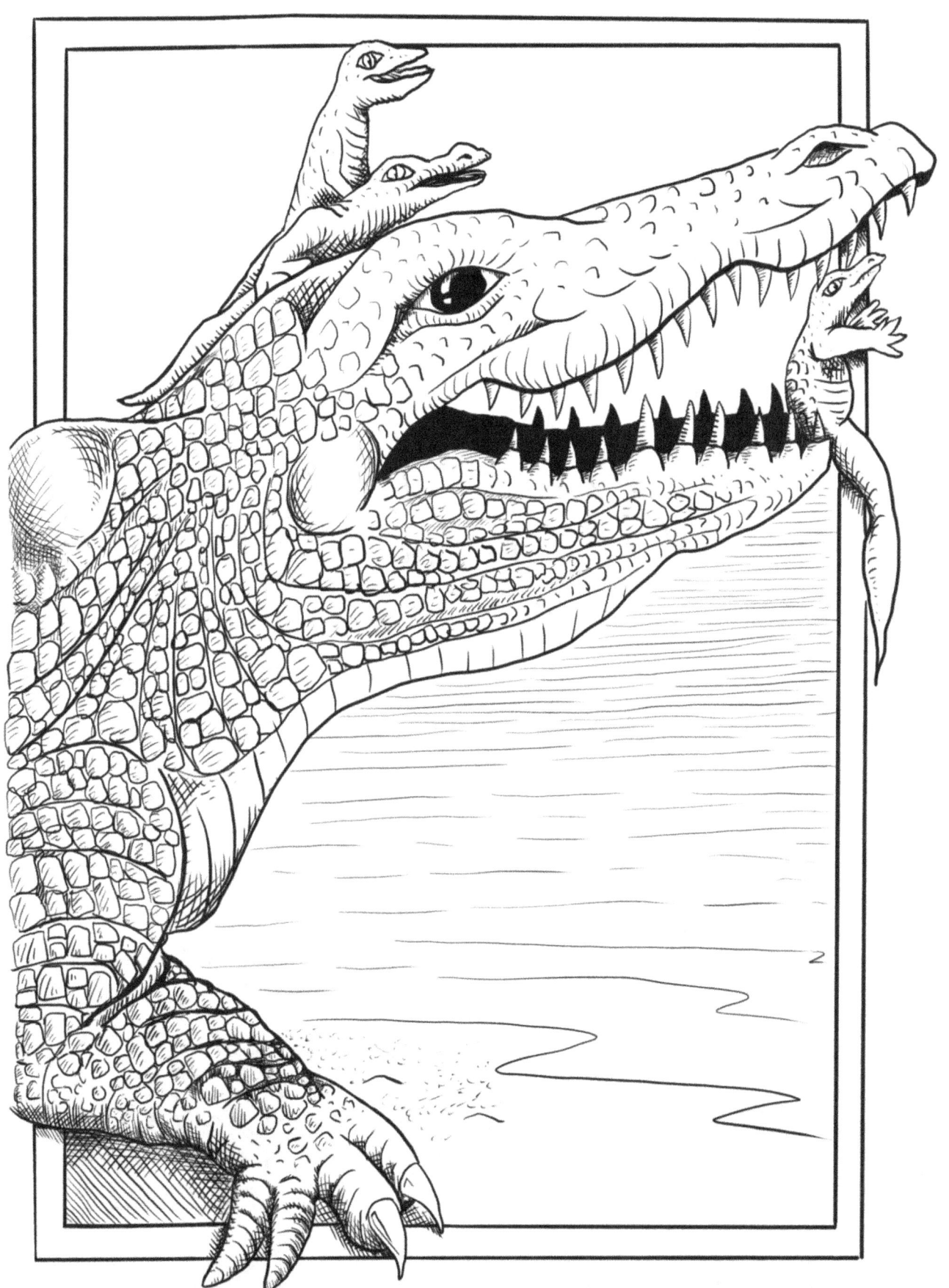

Hedgehogs
A SOW AND HER HOGLET

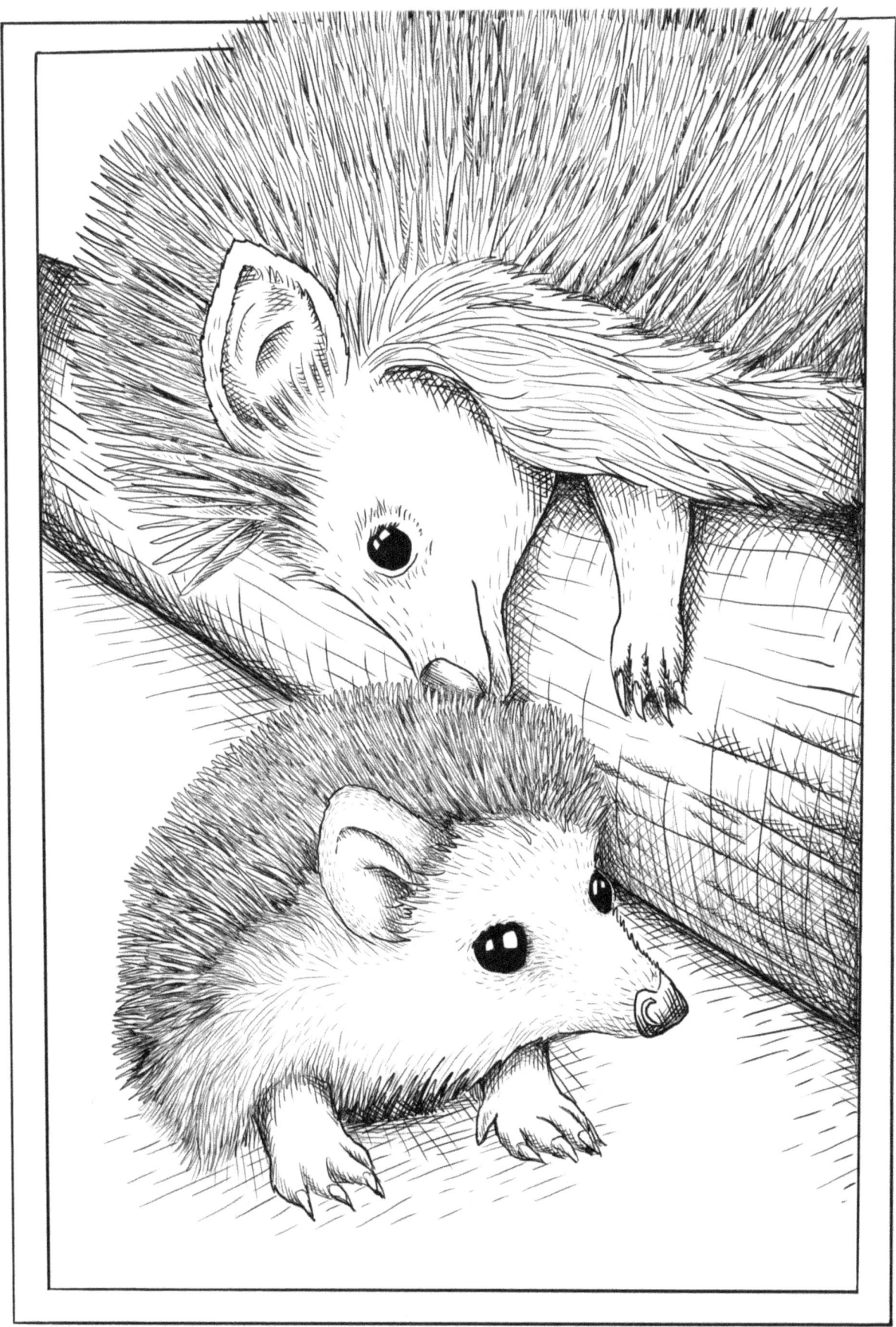

Frogs
A FROG AND HER FROGLET

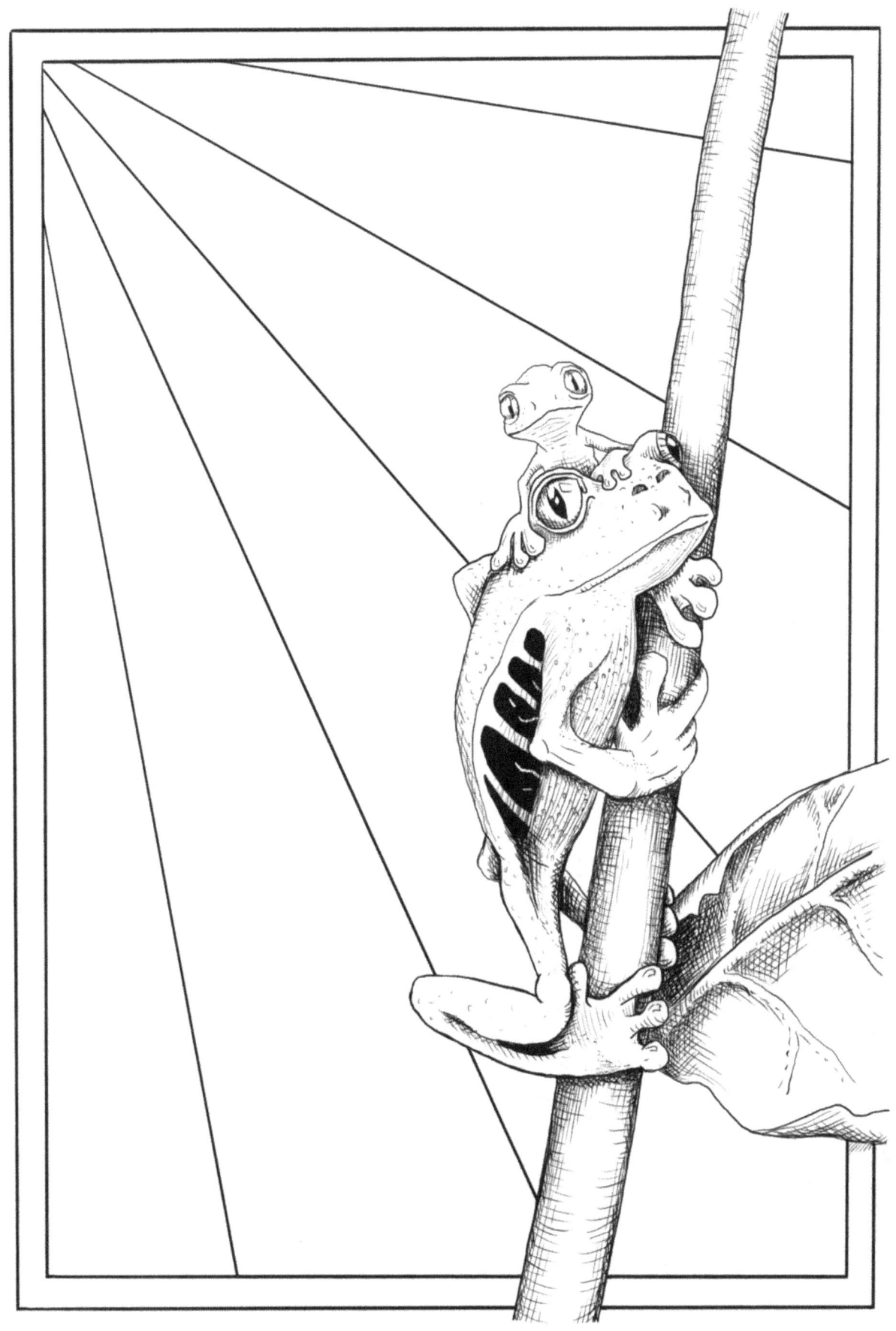

Armadillos
AN ARMADILLO AND HER PUP

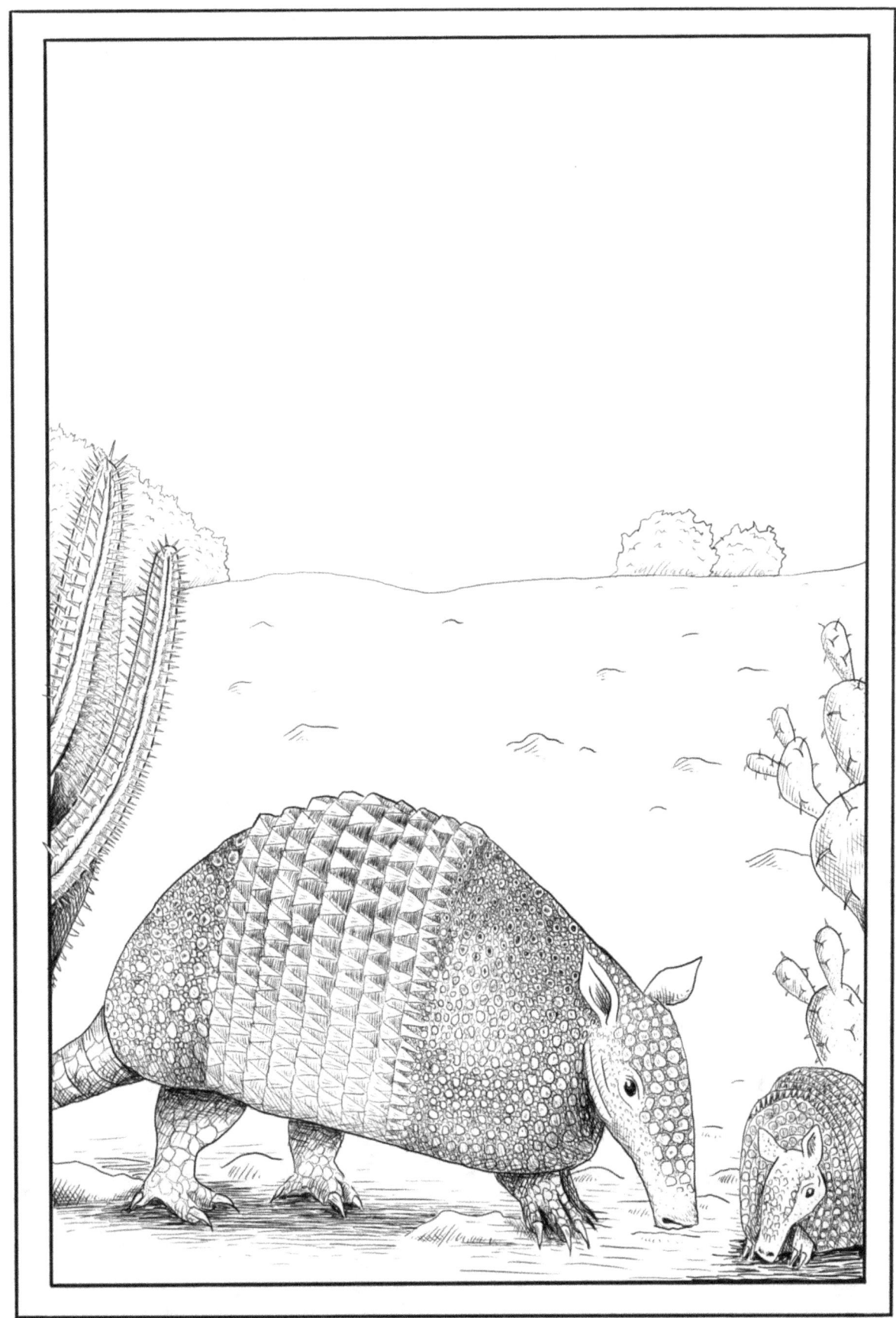

Llamas
A LLAMA AND HER CRIA

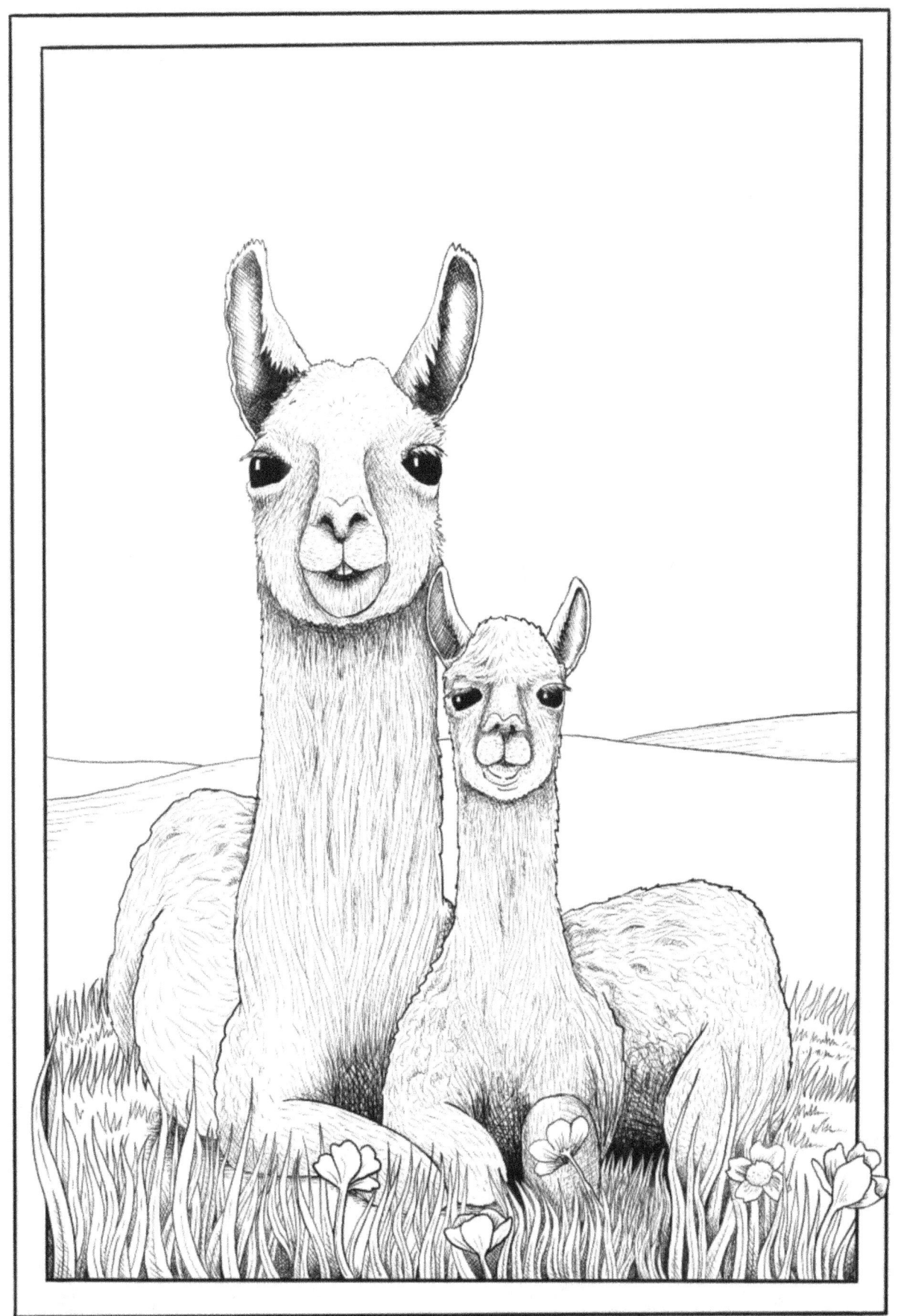

Swans
A PEN AND HER CYGNETS

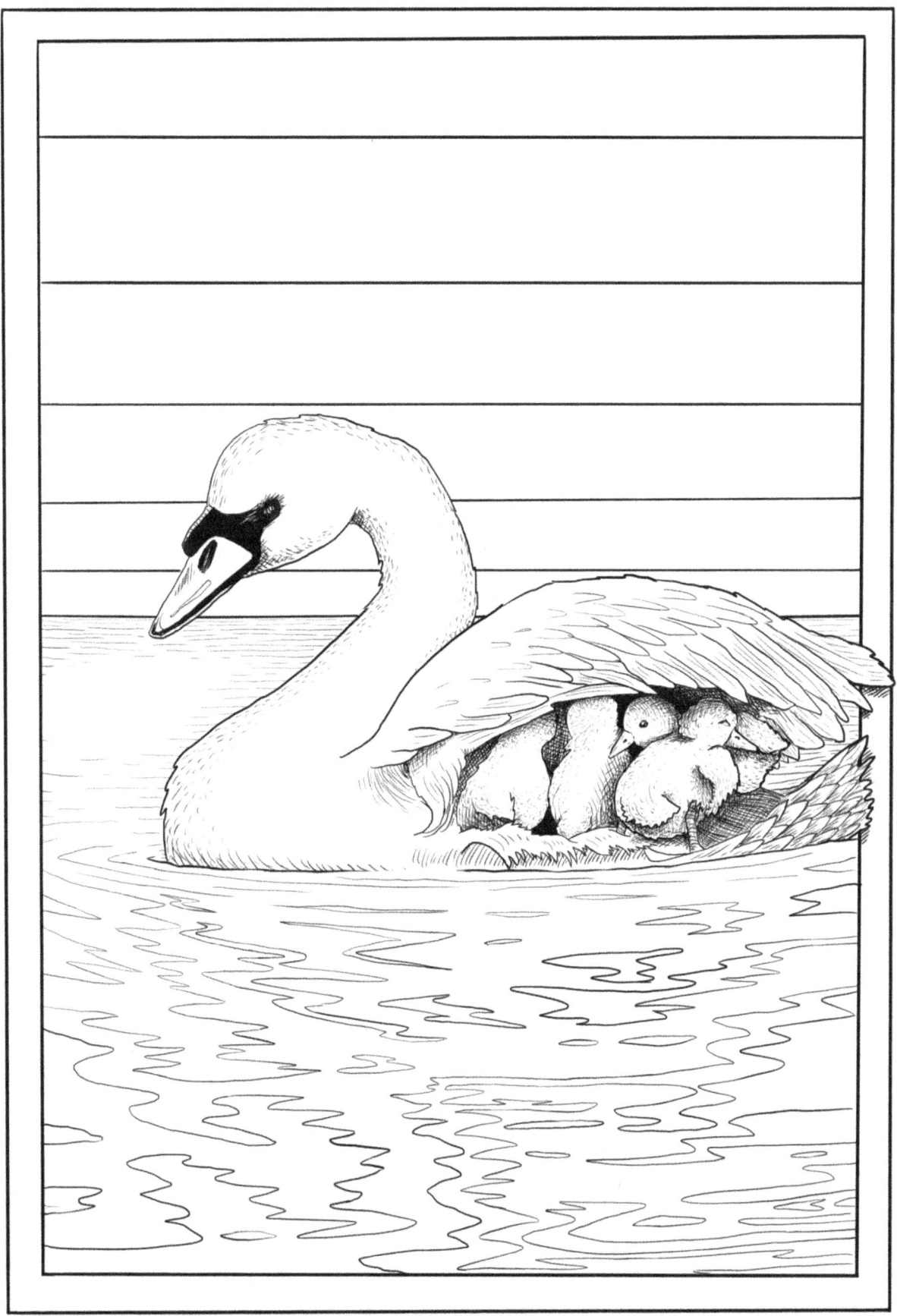

Kangaroos
A DOE AND HER JOEY

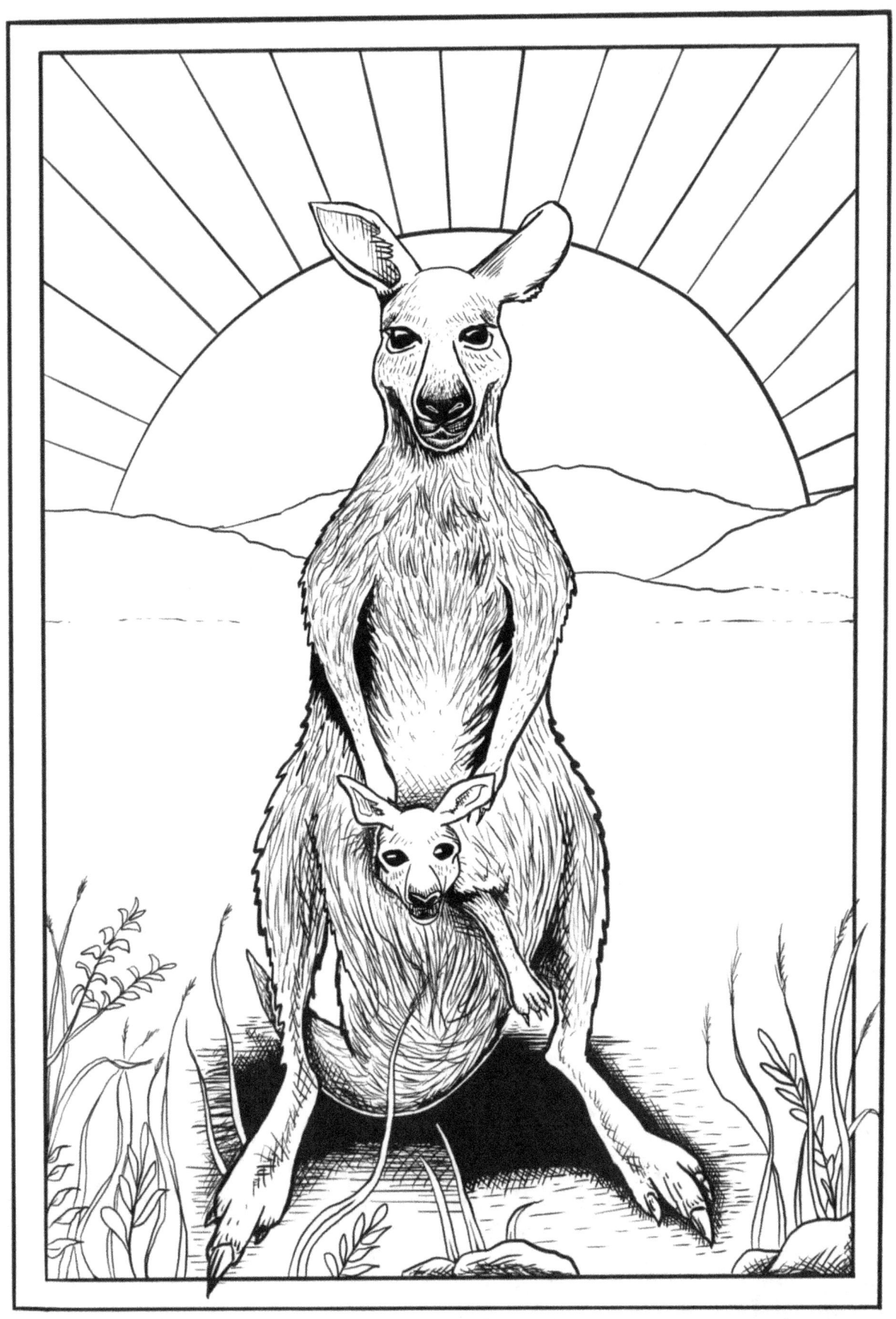

Koalas
A DOE AND HER JOEY

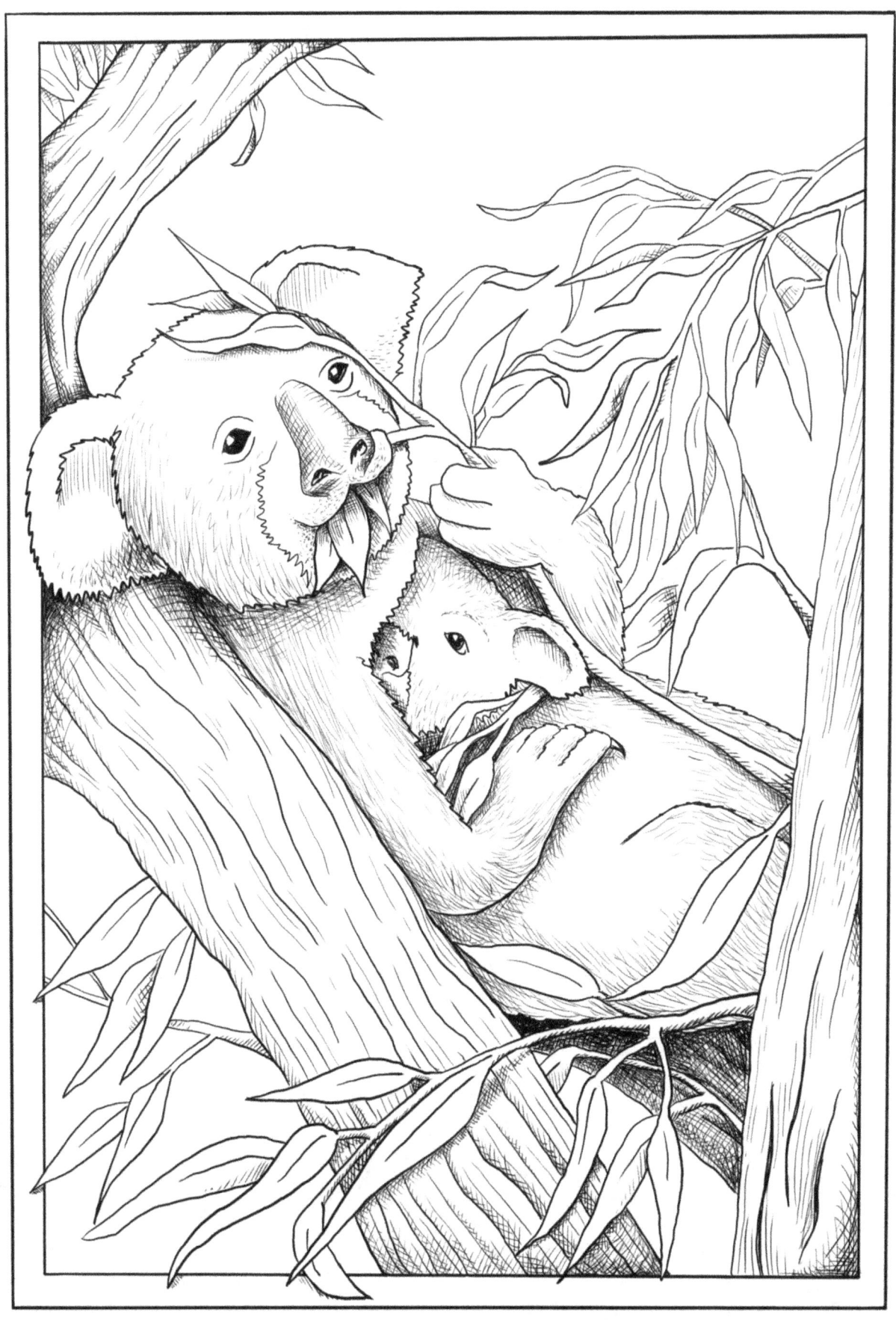

Quokkas
A QUOKKA AND HER JOEY

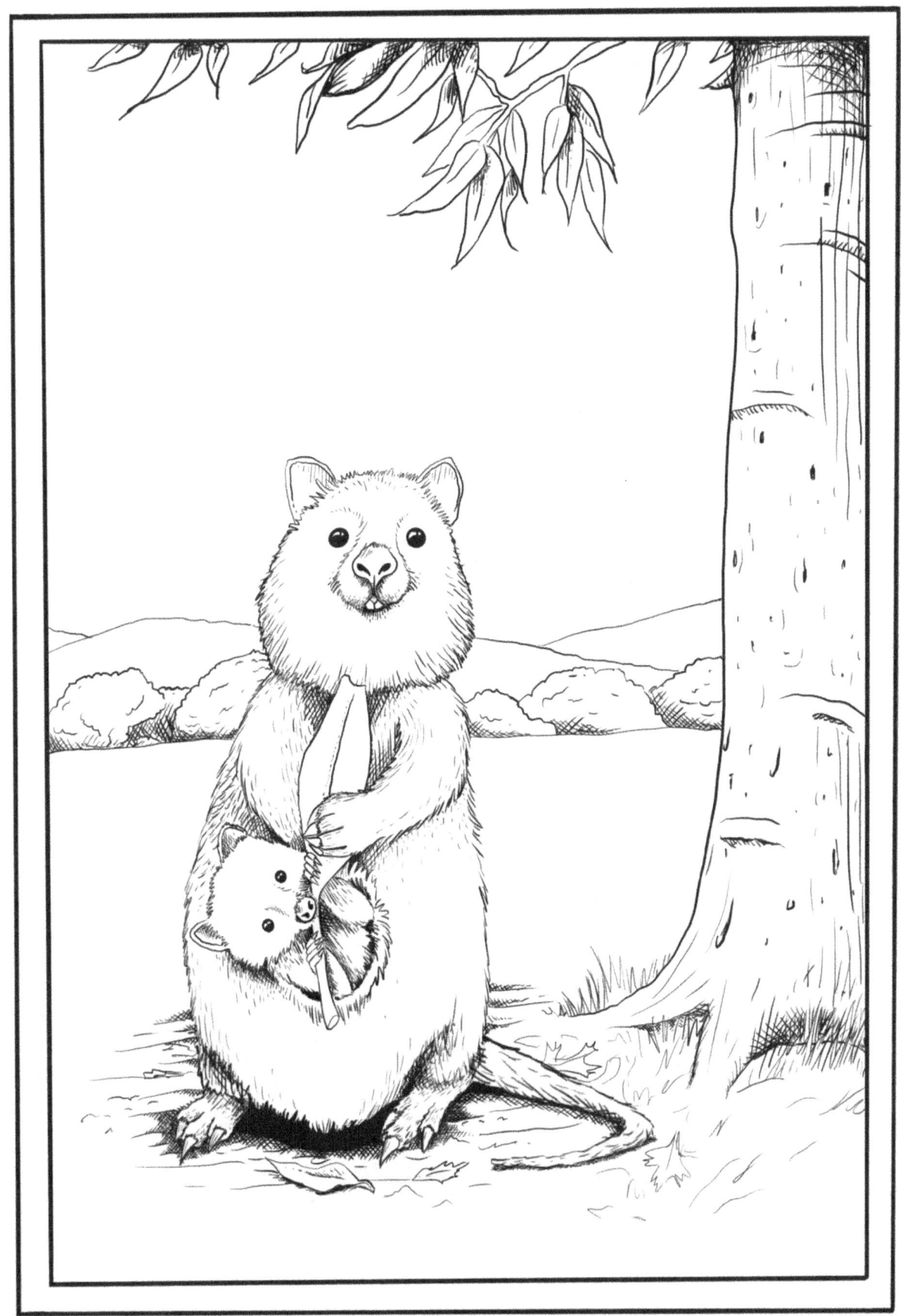

Sloths
A SOW AND HER CUB

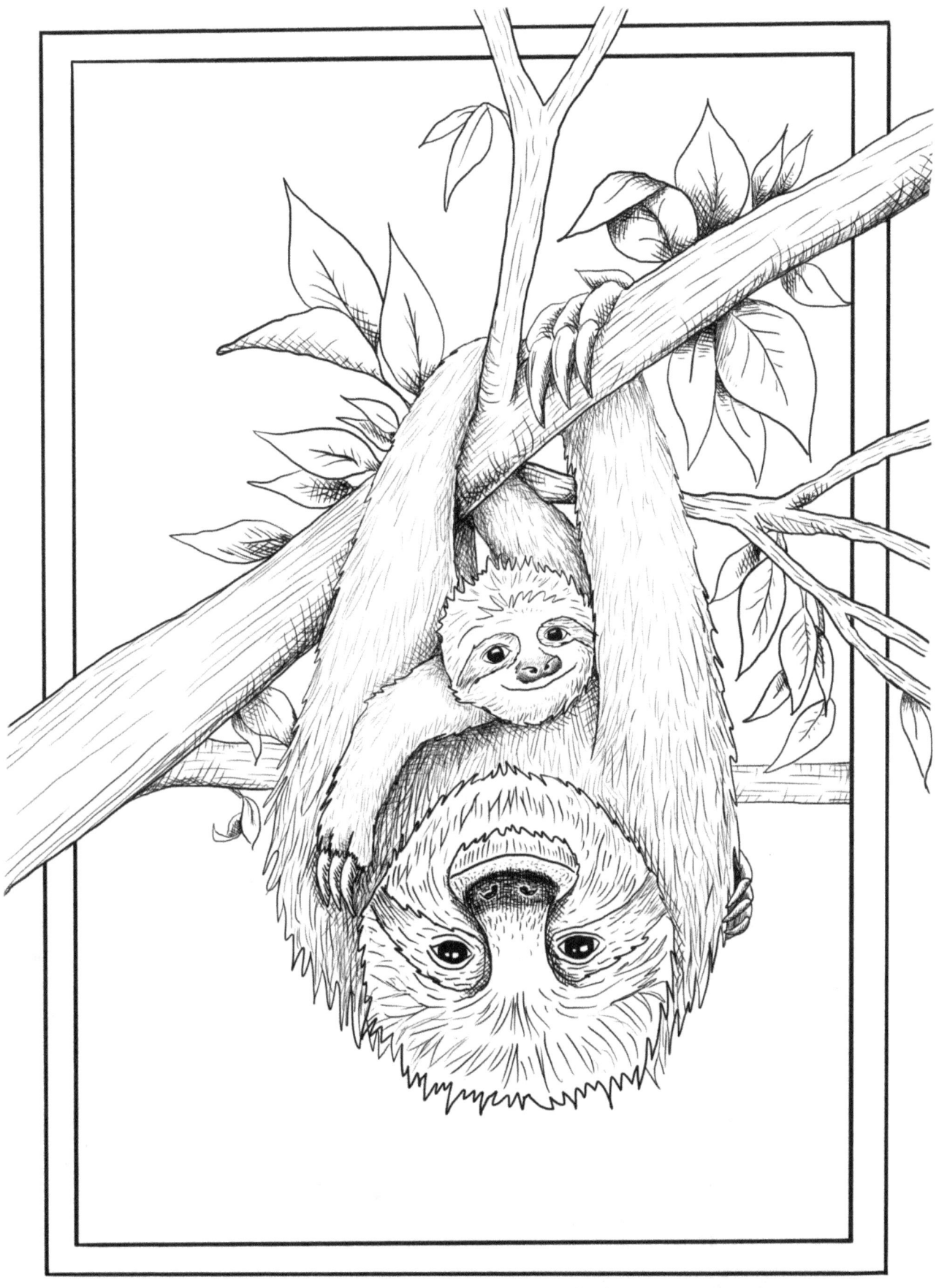

Camels
A COW AND HER CALF

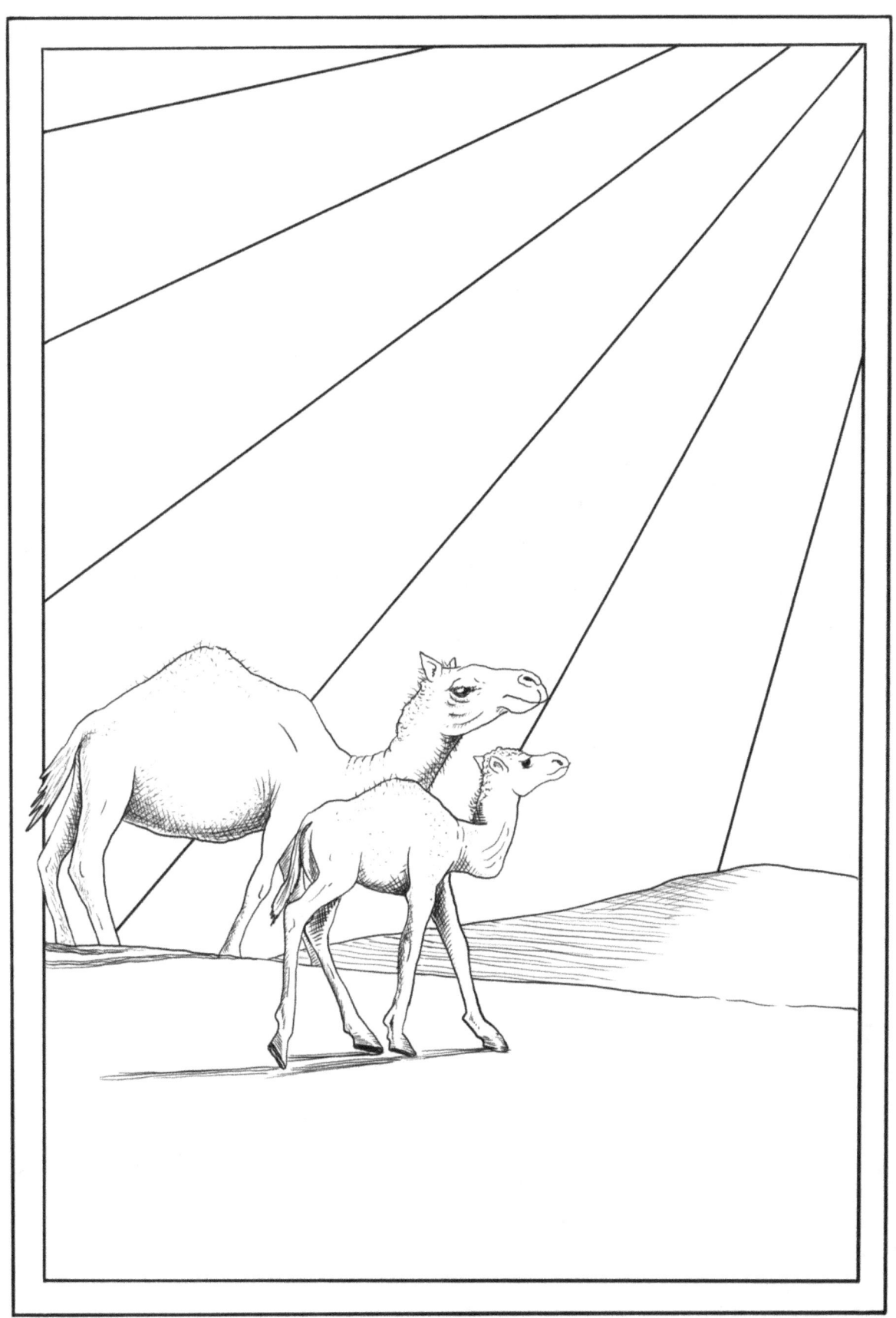

Platypuses
A PLATYPUS AND HER PUGGLE

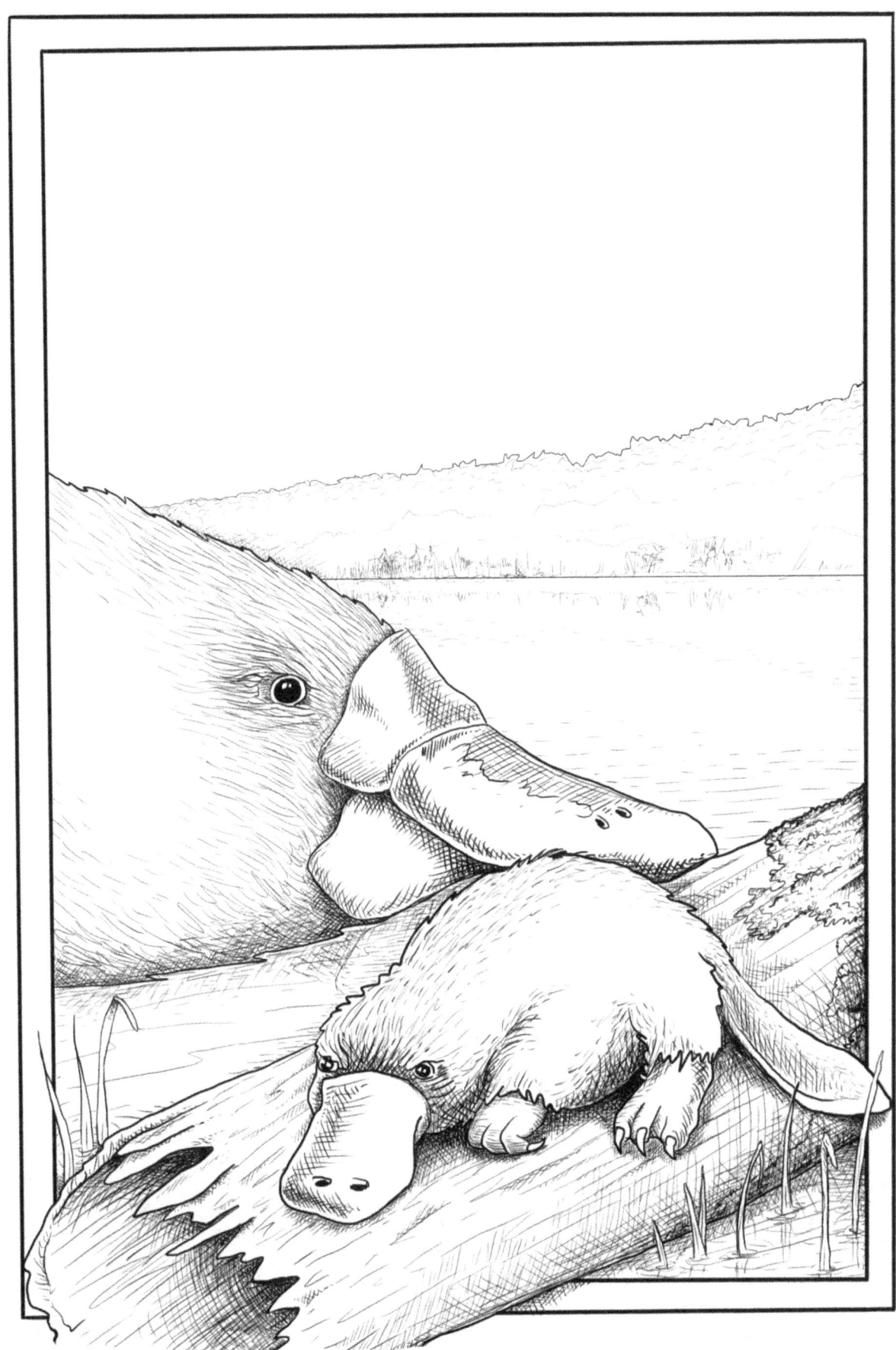

Red Pandas
A SOW AND HER CUB

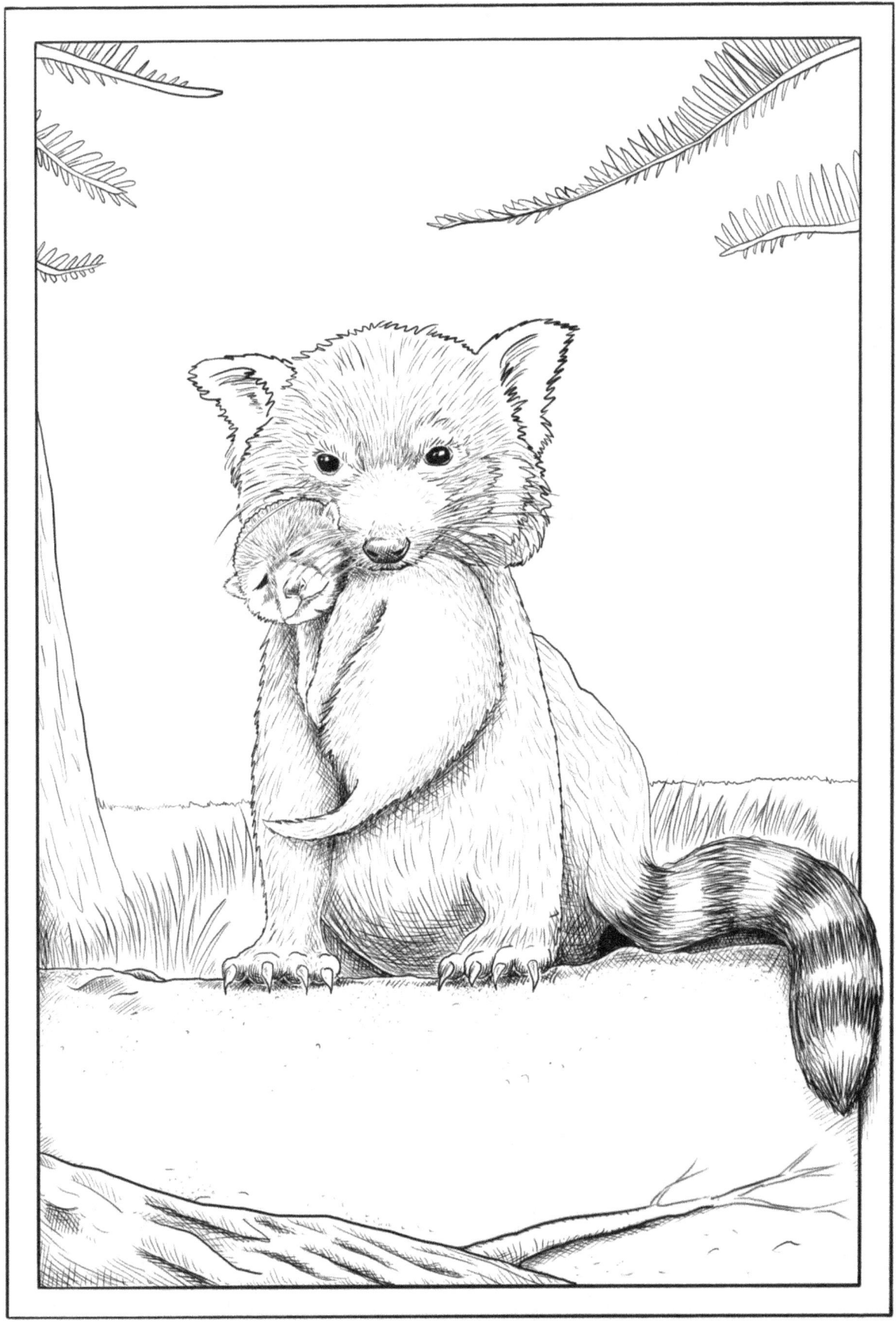

Reindeer
A COW AND HER CALF

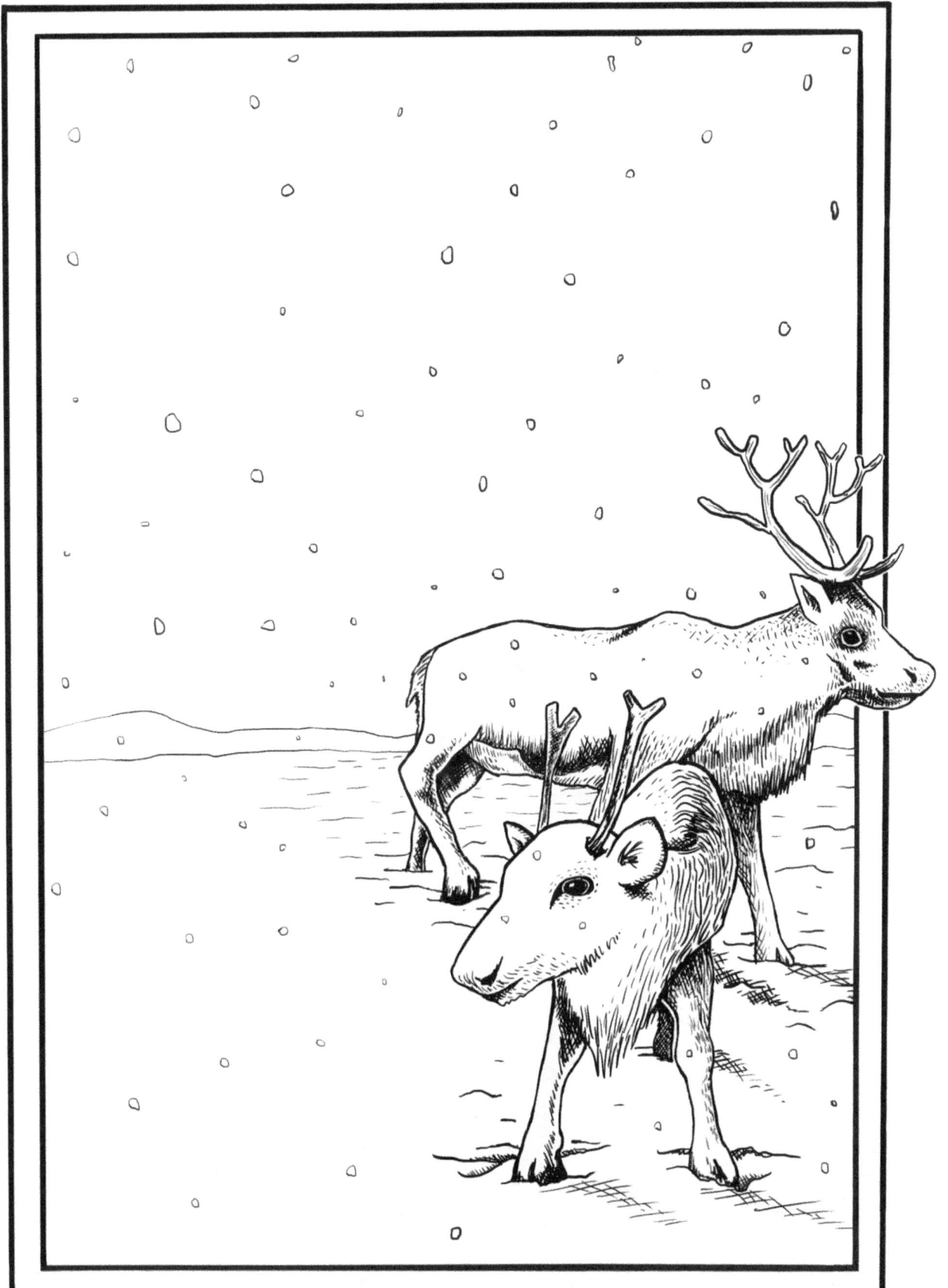

Penguins
A HEN AND HER CHICK

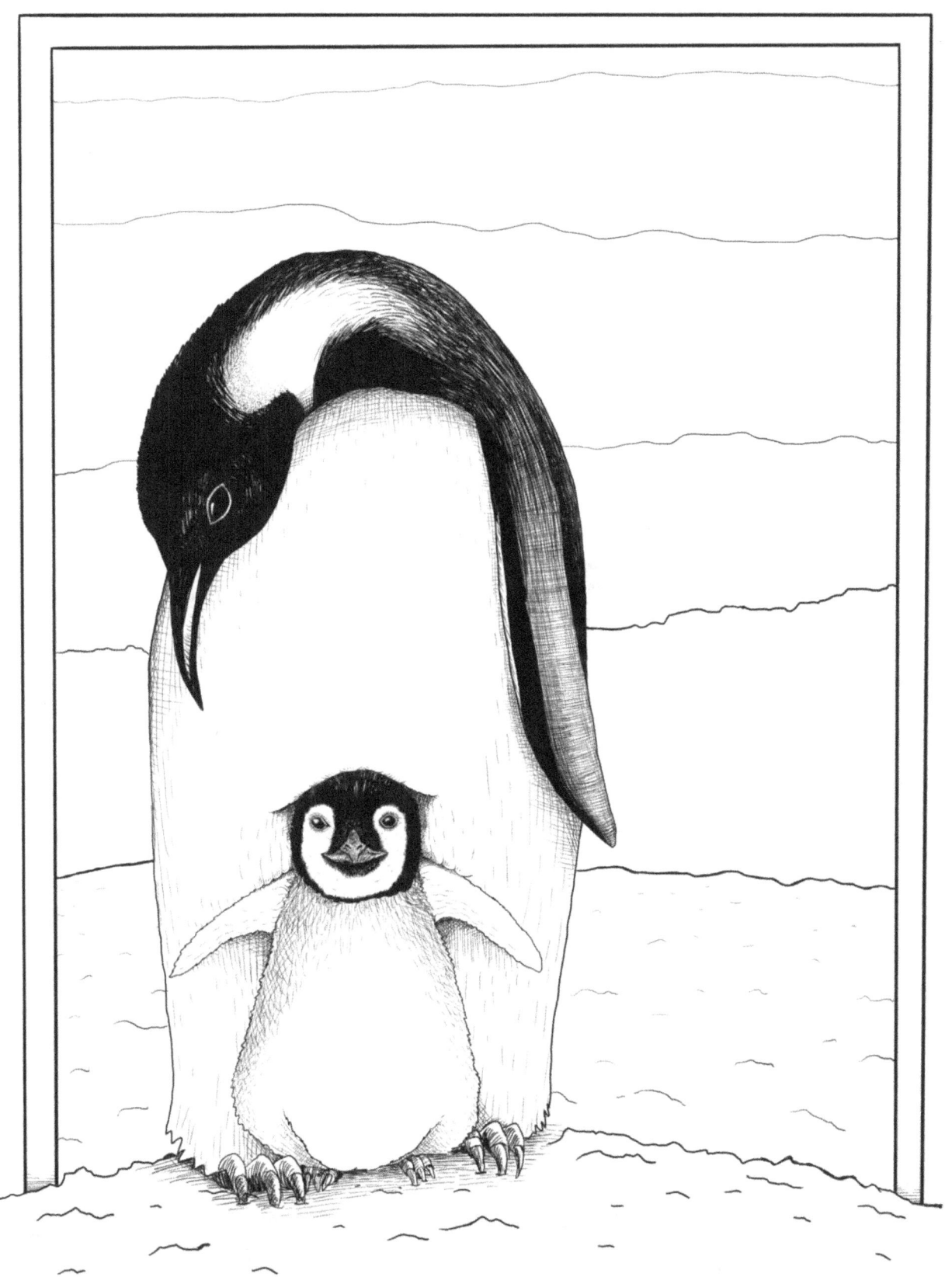

Bison
A COW AND HER CALF

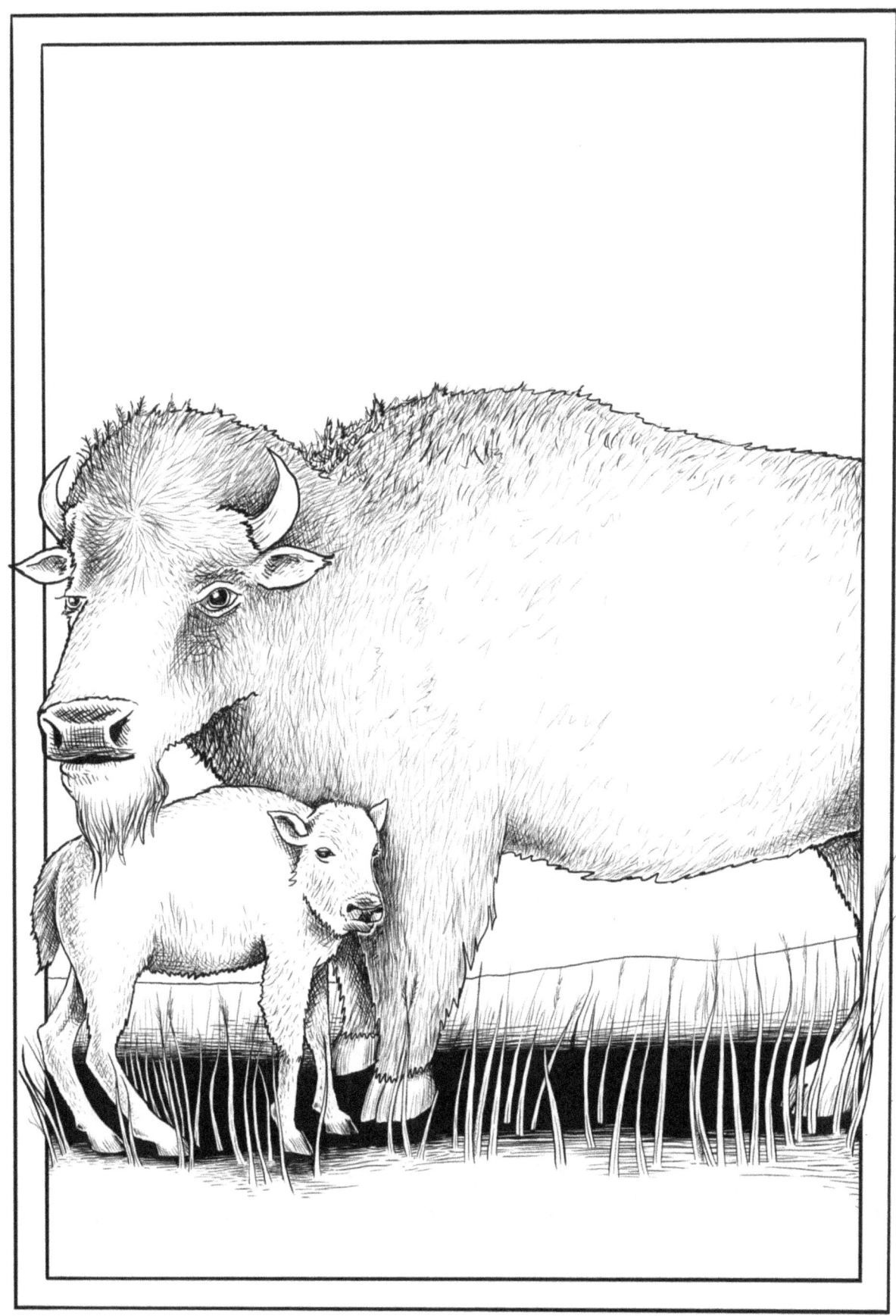

Rhinoceroses
A COW AND HER CALF

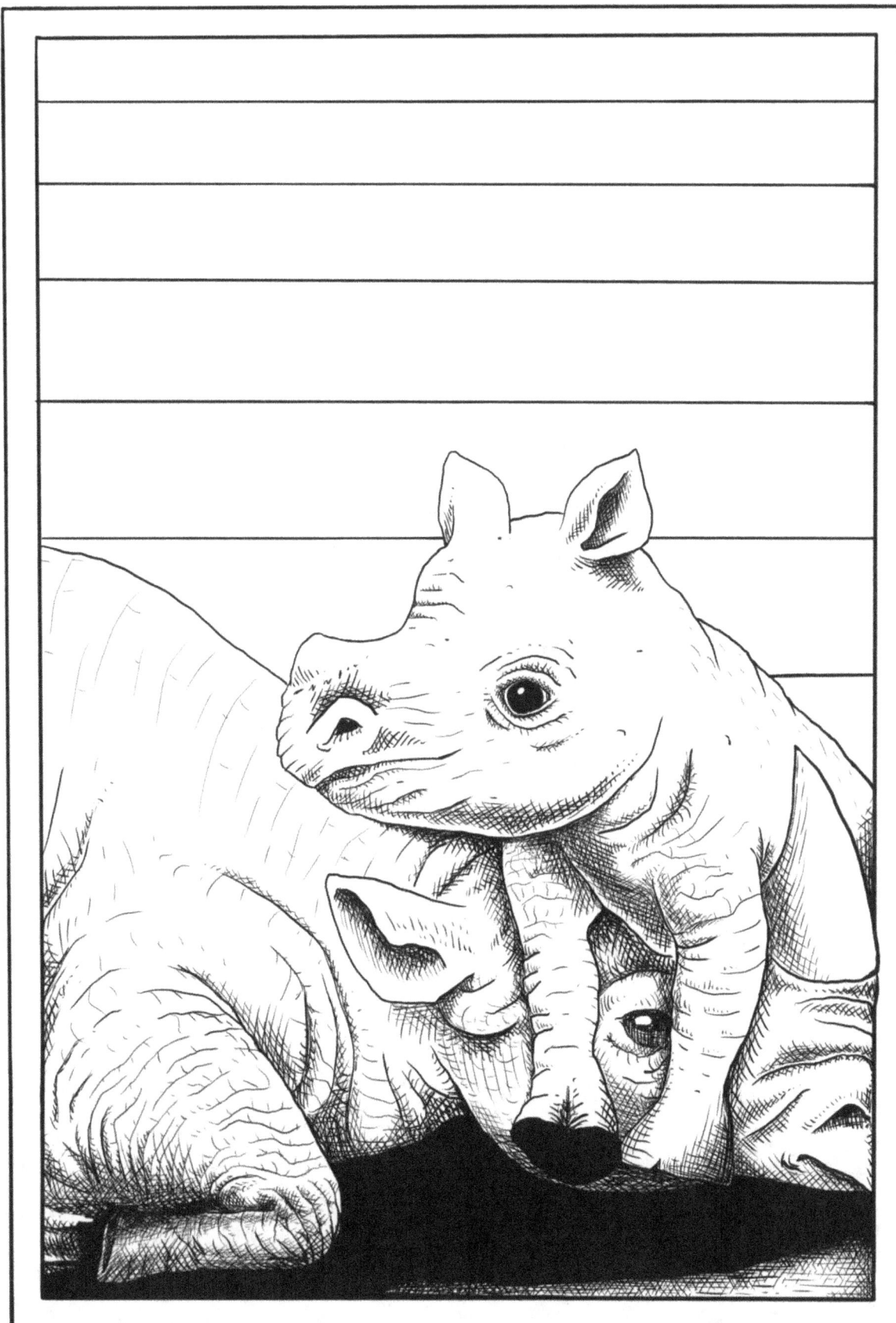

Pigeons
A HEN AND HER SQUAB

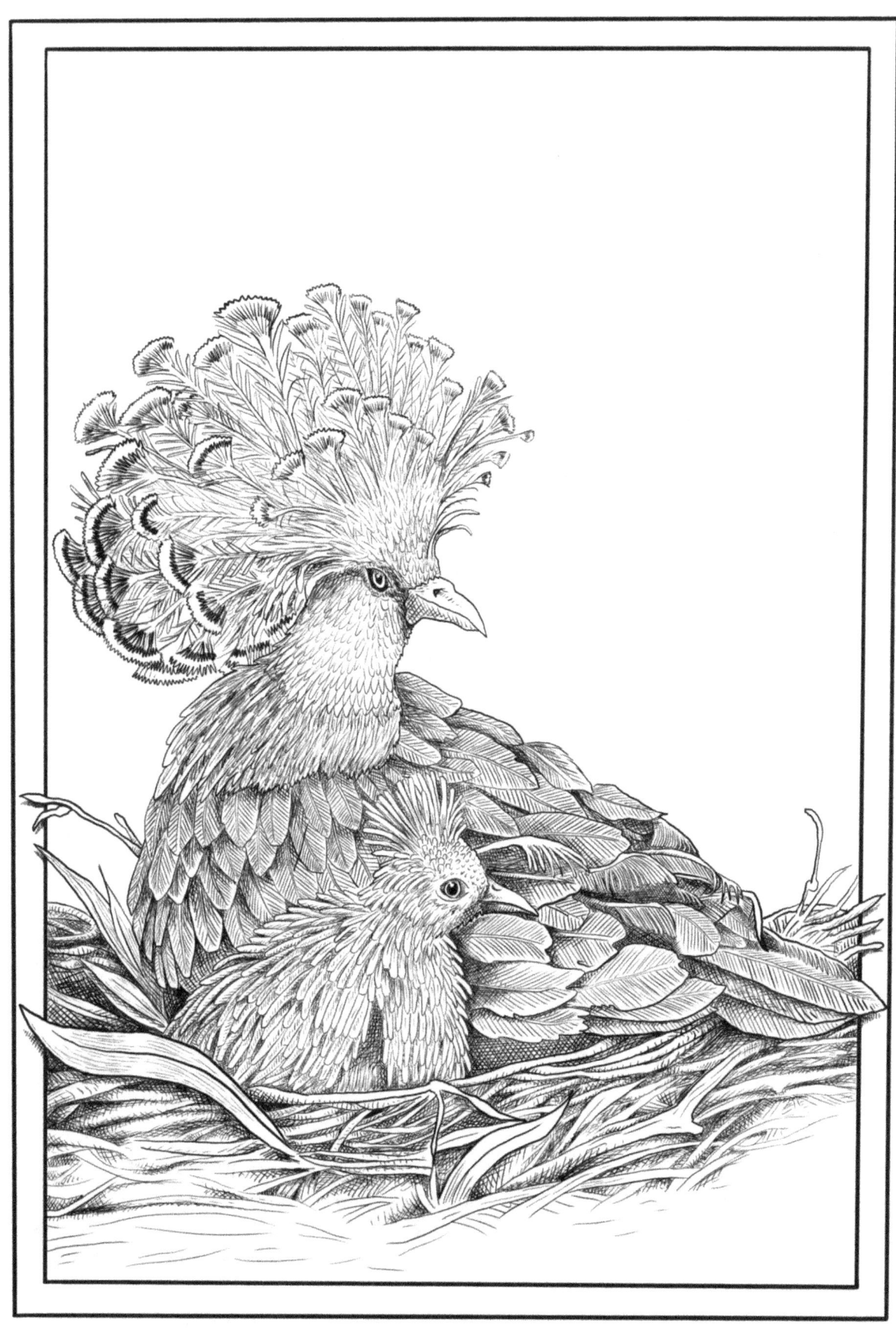

Petrels
A HEN AND HER CHICK

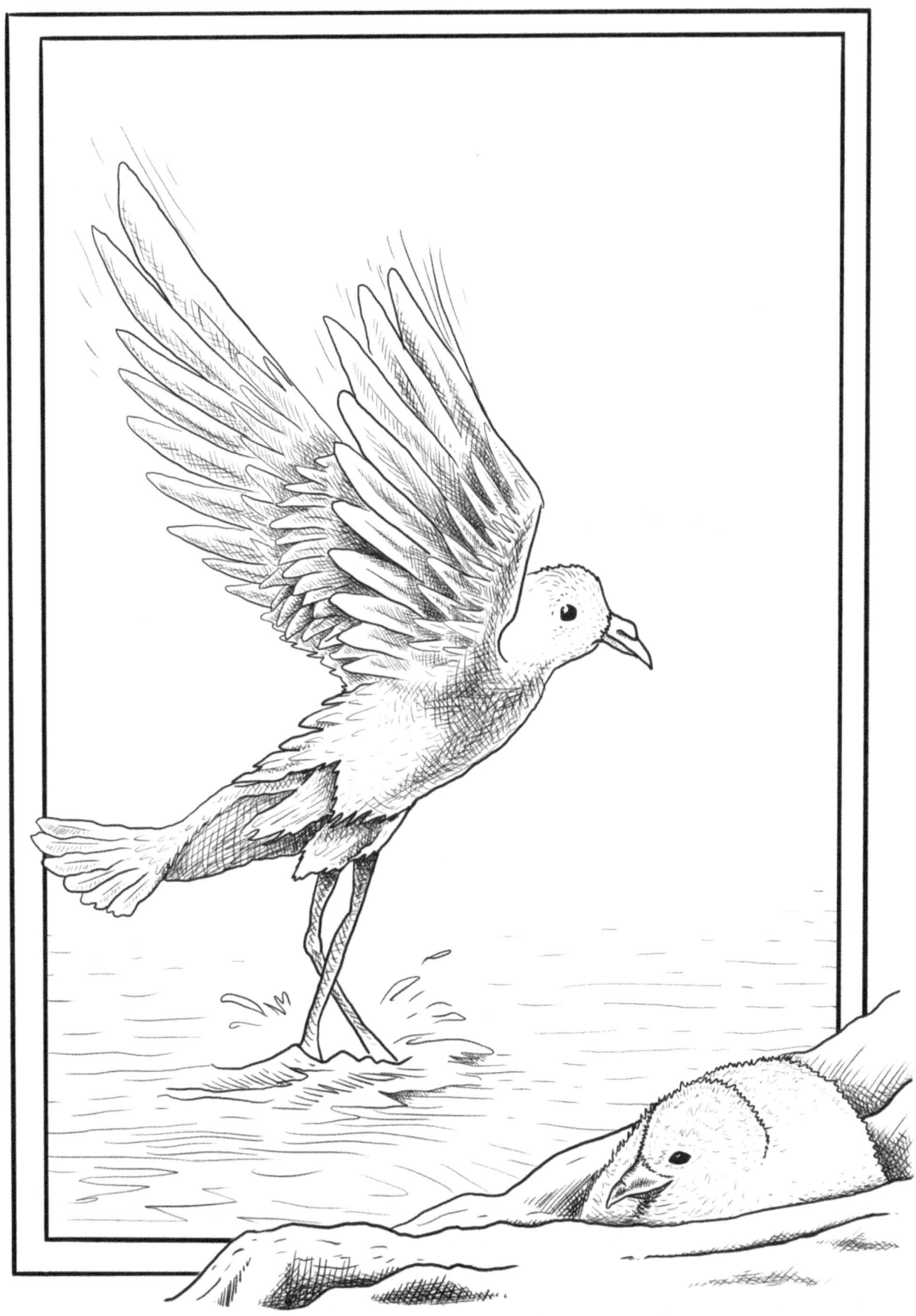

Chimpanzees
AN EMPRESS AND HER INFANTS

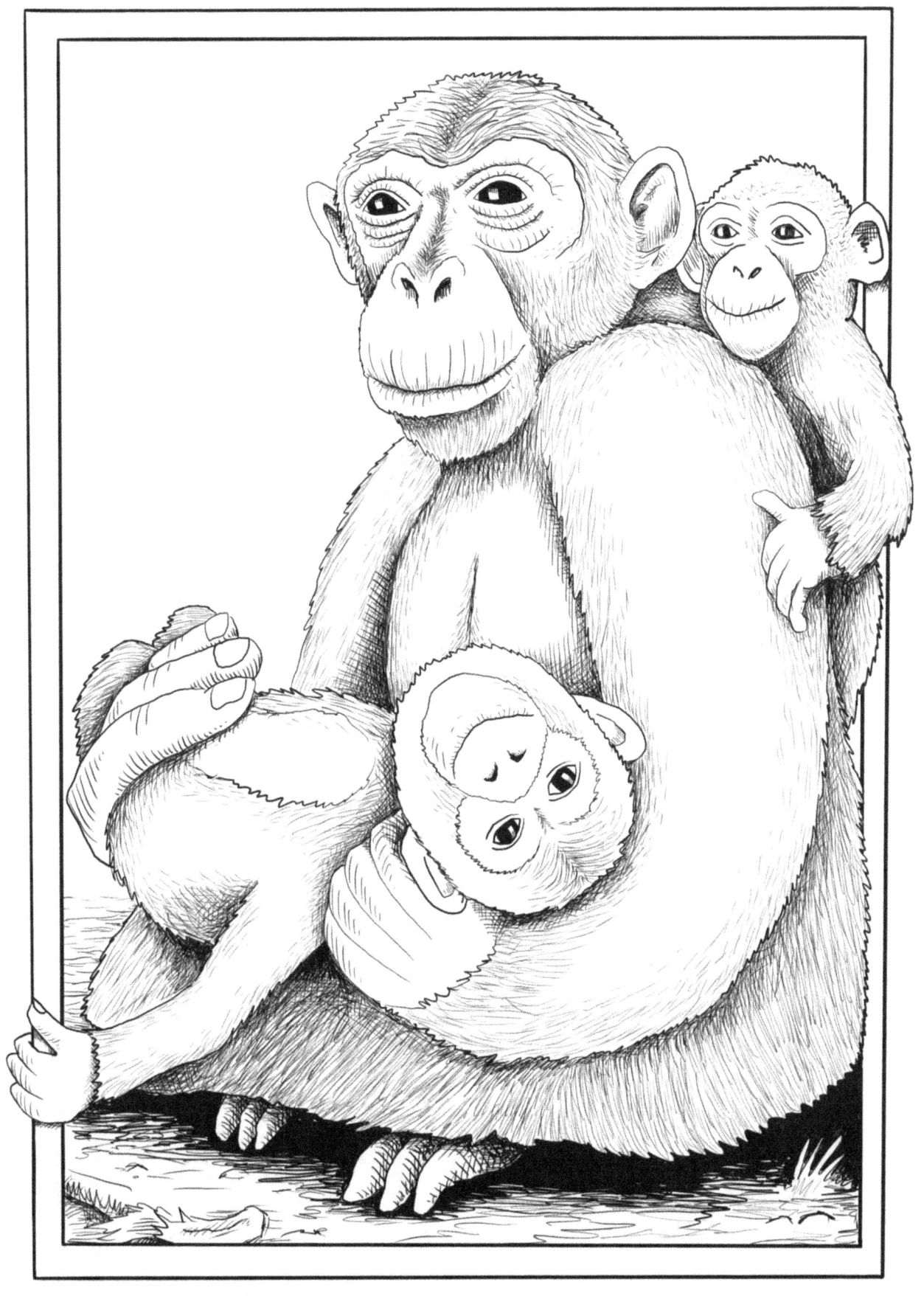

Elephants
A COW AND HER CALF

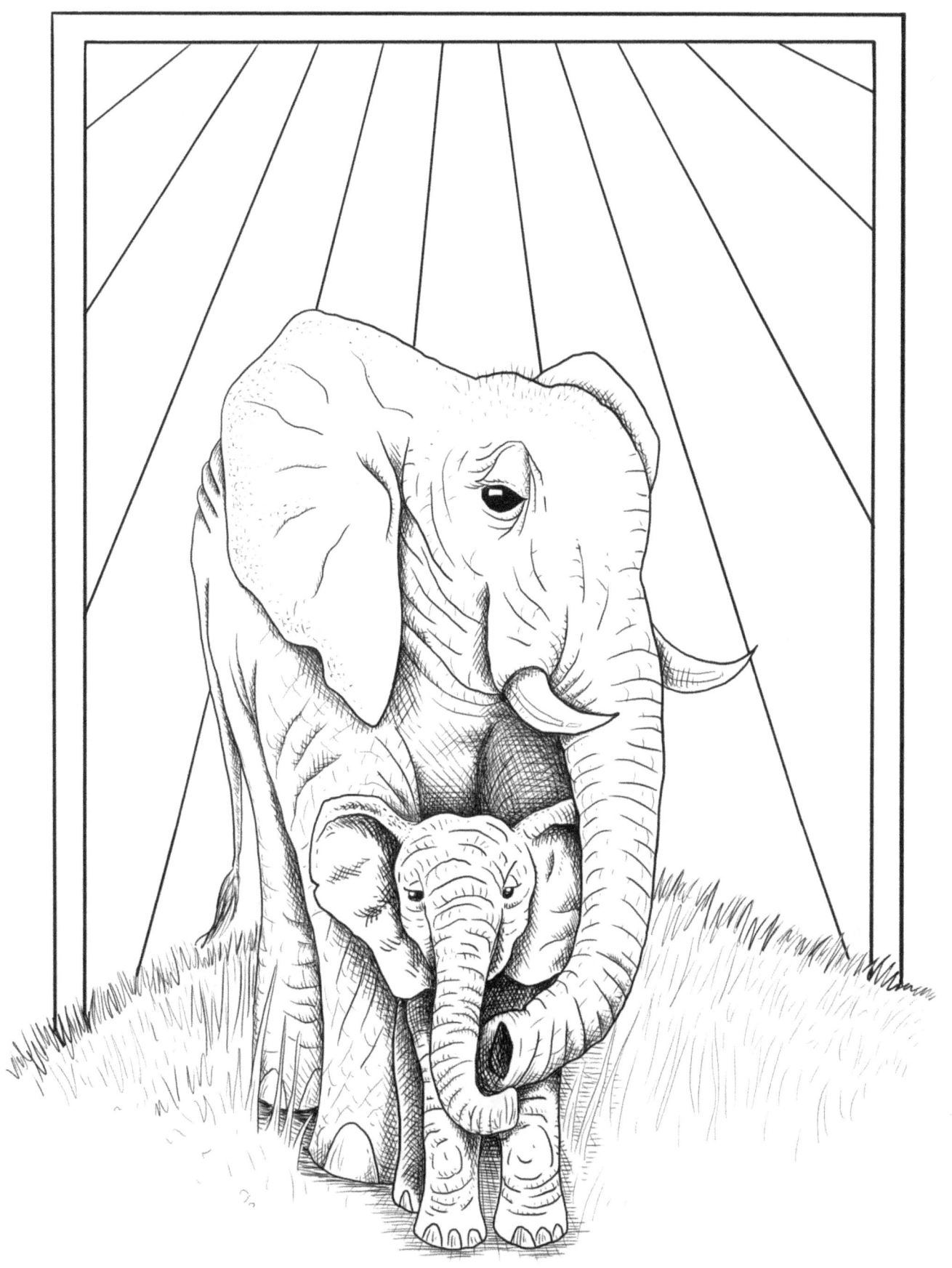

Giraffes
A COW AND HER CALF

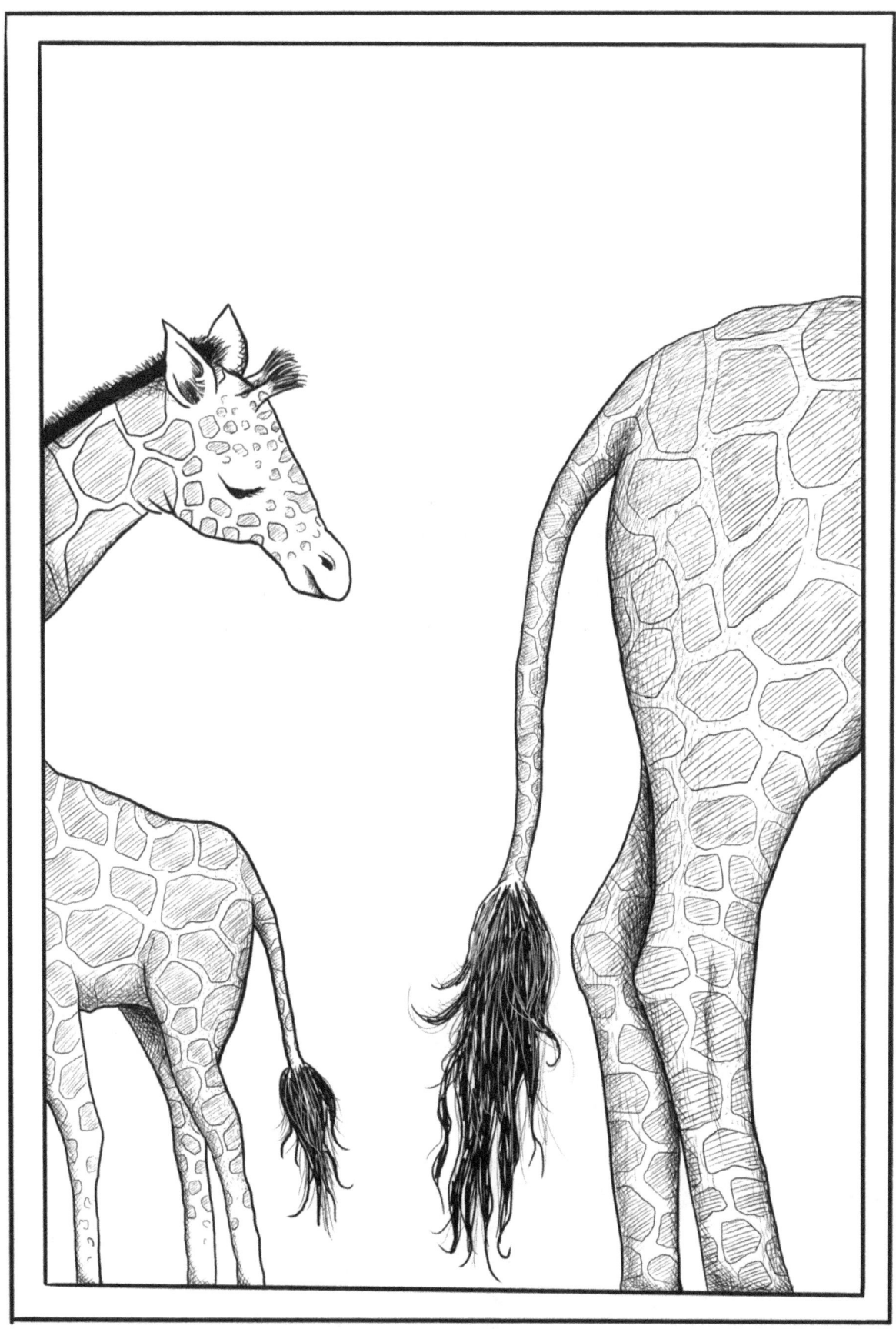

This book is dedicated to my wife Valerie, the mother of my children, and to my children - Zachary, Cherise, Braeden, and Viviana (who inspired this book when we found out we were expecting her).

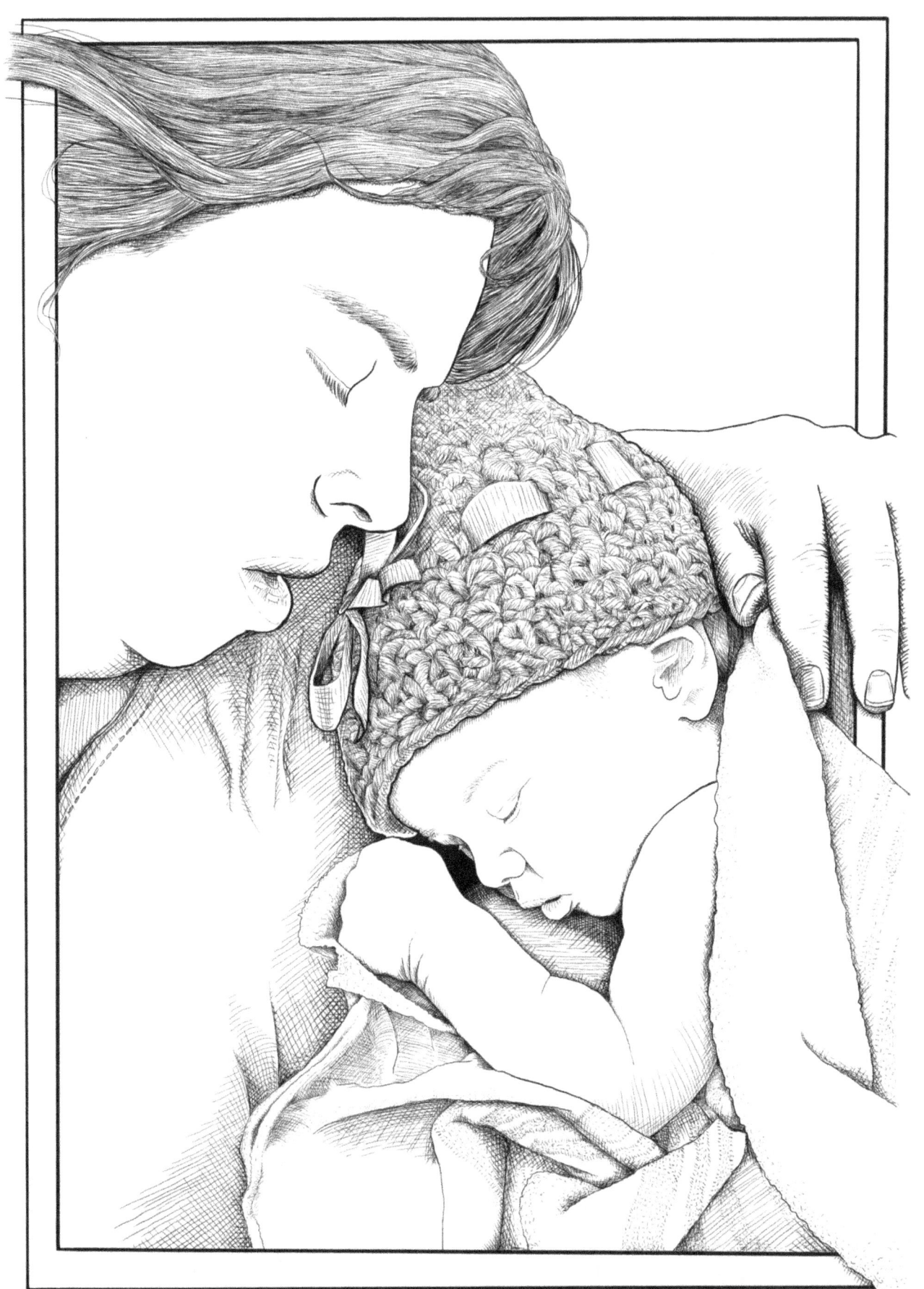

IT IS SOMETHING VERY SPECIAL,
JUST THE WAY GOD MADE IT TO BE.
GOD IS LOVE, AND IN HIS CREATION
HE DESIGNED A MIRACLE FOR ALL TO SEE.
THE MIRACLE OF BIRTH,
THE MIRACLE OF LIFE,
THE MIRACLE OF LOVE
IN A WORLD OF DARKNESS AND STRIFE.
AND THOUGH EVIL AND WICKEDNESS ABOUND
AND SO MUCH OF GOD'S CREATION
HAS BEEN DEFILED,
STILL SOMETHING REMAINS
THAT WILL ALWAYS ENDURE-
THAT IS THE LOVE
BETWEEN A MOTHER AND HER CHILD.

www.ingramcontent.com/pod-product-compliance
Lightning Source LLC
Chambersburg PA
CBHW081455220526
45466CB00008B/2650